Three men jumped out of the helicopter, and hurried toward a hump of soft dirt near the retaining wall. They took a quick look, then one of them turned and gave a thumbs-up sign to the passengers still in the helicopter. The pilot radioed the ground searchers that they had found the body.

Detective Bice was one of the first officers to reach the scene, and she squatted over the grave to scoop away a thin film of sand until she uncovered a flash of skin to further confirm a body was buried there. A few strands of golden blond hair, stiff with grime, were just below the dusty sprinkle of dirt at the top.

DEATH
OF A
MODEL

CLIFFORD L. LINEDECKER

St. Martin's Paperbacks

DEATH OF A MODEL

Copyright © 1997 by Clifford L. Linedecker.

Cover photographs courtesy Ramey Photo Agency (*left, middle*) and AP/Wide World Photos (*right*).

ISBN: 0-312-96163-4
EAN: 9780312-96163-3

Printed in the United States of America

St. Martin's Paperbacks edition/April 1997

10 9 8 7 6 5 4 3 2

Dedication

To all the models and aspiring models out there: Good luck, have fun, be careful.

Acknowledgments

Books dealing with true events aren't created solely through the efforts of authors, but require the cooperation and input of many people.

Two of the people I owe thanks to for their help with this book are John Coll Metcalfe, of the *News-Pilot* in San Pedro, California; and Greg Sowinski, a senior journalism student at Ohio State University and reporter for the campus newspaper, *The Lantern.*

Coll went that extra mile digging through a blizzard of court documents and filtering out the best for me during the rapidly developing legal proceedings in Los Angeles. He was also my "eyes and ears" in Los Angeles after I was required by a fast-approaching deadline to move from the role of active researcher to writer.

Greg conducted interviews and dug up vital information about Charles Rathbun's early life in and around Columbus, Ohio. His contacts and knowledge of the Columbus area were a great help, and he impressed me with his industry and innovativeness. I expect him to mold a fine career for himself in journalism.

Thanks also to the helpful folks with the Los Angeles Sheriff's Department's Media Relations Bureau who were courteous and helpful; the Lansing Public Library in Lansing, Michigan, for their efficient and cheerful assistance; and to many others who were quick to share information and insight into the story.

A special note of appreciation is due to Charles Spicer, my editor at St. Martin's Press, for suggesting the book and for his confidence in me. Thanks also to my agent, Tony Seidl of T. D. Media, for his help in guiding me through the morass of contracts and other matters dealing with the business side of the project.

The account presented here is as true and factual as it is possible to make it, based on interviews, documents, personal observation, and other sources available to me. In order to smooth out the narrative and make the story more readable, slight changes have been made in the chronology of the murder suspect's interrogation by police.

But no names have been changed, no conversation made up, and dates, places, and events are all presented here exactly as they occurred or were reported by participants and other witnesses.

Contents

"Everybody should be lucky and have a daughter like that."

Mrs. Elaine Sobek, to:
Los Angeles Daily News

"I always considered myself very fortunate because Chuck never used drugs and was never convicted of anything."

H. Robert Rathbun,
Father of suspect, to:
The Columbus Dispatch

Introduction

It's not uncommon to hear professional modeling described as the kind of job a girl would die for.

Obviously, the innocently expressed observation isn't meant to be taken literally.

But it can happen. It happened to Linda Elaine Sobek, a young woman who was as full of sunshine and as sparkling bright as the fine white sandy beaches that line the oceanside communities of Los Angeles County's South Bay where she grew up, played, and built a rewarding career for herself as a successful cheesecake model.

Linda died a nasty death, and the ugliness followed her to the grave. At this writing the modern tragedy was still playing itself out in the criminal courts.

Her story as it's recounted here isn't meant to frighten anyone away from considering a modeling career for themselves. Professional modeling, whether it's pursued on the runways of the international fashion industry, hostessing at conventions and trade shows, or posing for magazine covers and calendar pinups can be wonderfully exciting and tremendously gratifying for any young woman.

Competing with peers in the demanding profession can build self-esteem, sophistication, and grace as well as dazzling financial rewards. Modeling is hard work, however, and physical beauty alone, or as Linda said in classic politically correct phraseology—"being genetically gifted"—isn't enough to ensure success.

Good models must be ambitious, industrious, disciplined, and equipped with good common sense if they expect to make a living for themselves in the demanding trade. Linda Sobek had all of those qualities.

She was also sufficiently experienced and knowledgeable to be cautious; but a last-minute photo shoot cost the lovely blond model her life.

Like Linda, Charles Edgar Rathbun was a native of Los Angeles County who also built a successful career for himself in a glamorous profession. Rathbun became a photographer, specializing in pictures of new cars and trucks—often using lovely young female models in bikinis or cutoffs and tops as eye-catching props.

The talented shutterbug had an enviable ability to elevate automobile and cheesecake photography to a fine art. His romantic life was less rewarding.

His personality was about as different from Linda's as it could be. He was temperamental, often outspokenly critical of the models he worked with, and given to loud outbursts of anger. He was also a decade older than the California beauty and spent his teenage and early adult years in the Midwest. Finally when he returned to his roots in the Golden State he carried along an embarrassing secret, a long-ago brush with the law.

Linda was loving and outgoing. She made new friends easily, diligently cultivated old friendships, and treasured her relationship with her family. If she had doubts or criticisms of someone, she was most likely to keep the negative thoughts to herself or to confine them to the privacy of her diary.

She was a Golden Girl, but even Golden Girls have flaws, and Linda's desperate desire for others to return the love she gave so openly created troubling ripples in the otherwise mirror-smooth quiescence of her life. Despite all her friends and professional success, there were times when she could be as vulnerable as a wounded fawn.

Yet, when her path crossed with that of Charles Rathbun, the consequence was a lethal episode of violence and tragedy. The lives of the temperamental freelance photographer and the charming beach bunny and body model became inextricably and forever linked.

DEATH
OF A
MODEL

PROLOGUE

NOVEMBER 16, 1995

Linda Sobek was the kind of daughter who was every parent's dream.

She was picture pretty, and in fact the shapely blue-eyed blonde was so attractive that she had forged a successful career for herself as a calendar and swimsuit model.

The twenty-seven-year-old woman's beauty was more than skin-deep, however, and family, friends, and other acquaintances agreed she was as lovely inside as outside. Kindness and consideration for others, along with a sunny, upbeat disposition, were linchpins of her character and personality.

She was especially close to her family, and although she lived only a few miles away from the home of her parents in the Los Angeles suburb of Lakewood—a short distance inland from San Pedro Bay—she made short chats with her mother a daily habit.

The five foot four inch, 105-pound, size three model kept a busy schedule, and this day in November was no exception. She already had appointments booked throughout the day and into the early evening when her mother, Elaine, telephoned at about 10:45 Thursday morning. Linda chatted for a few moments before cutting the conversation short.

She explained she was running late and was in a hurry for a meeting with a photographer named Chuck. A modeling shoot was set up for a car magazine. Later in the day she had an appointment for a costume fitting for a bit part on the popular television series, *Married With Children*, as well as a couple of other commitments.

Linda promised her mother she would call back later in the day to talk over plans for a weekend barbecue. After the hurried good-bye, she dictated a quick message for her paging service advising callers they had reached "Linda," that it was 11 A.M., Thursday, and she expected to spend the rest of the day on location. She explained she wouldn't have access to a telephone and asked callers to leave a message, which she would reply to that evening.

Either just before or moments after dictating the telephone message, she also made another call canceling a luncheon date at the Cafe Med restaurant on trendy Sunset Boulevard in Hollywood. She was going to be tied up with the photo shoot.

A few minutes later the vibrant young model stepped out the door of the big four-bedroom house she shared with three roommates on the corner of Third Street and Beach in Hermosa Beach, and into the brilliant Southern California sunshine. Dressed in a crisply clean top and a pair of snappy shorts, she was in such a hurry that curlers were still in place in her corn-silk yellow hair. Climbing into her spiffy white Nissan 240 SX sports coupe, she steered the car into the street.

Linda Sobek never showed up for the costume fitting or for the other appointments later in the day. And she never called her mother back to firm up the plans for the weekend barbecue.

ONE

A Missing Person

Linda Sobek appeared to have simply vanished from the face of the earth.

She missed every one of her afternoon appointments and never showed up for the evening off-camera rehearsal to work out poses for a calendar featuring clothing styles from the 1940s. She missed other sittings the next day, and a photo shoot scheduled the following Monday.

She wasn't waiting at the Los Angeles International Airport for her boyfriend on Friday when he arrived on a flight from Las Vegas so they could spend the weekend together as previously planned.

And Linda never returned to the spacious house a short walk from the ocean, which she had lived in for about six months. She had moved there from her parents' home to spread her wings and make it on her own.

Her mother became worried after Linda failed to return the promised call. Mrs. Sobek telephoned one of her daughter's closest friends, Brooke Morales, and told her Linda was missing. Brooke and Linda were the same age and shared many common interests including modeling. They were such close friends, Linda said, that she felt like they were sisters. Aware of how out of character it was for Linda not to keep in touch with her mother, Brooke did some checking on her friend and learned she missed three scheduled appointments Thursday.

The missing woman was especially enthusiastic about the costume fitting for the popular television show *Married With Children*. She had lined up a small part on the Fox sitcom and was hopeful it would lead to a breakthrough for her as an actress. Linda was dependable and firmly devoted to her career, and it was inconceivable that she would deliberately miss the fitting without even bothering to telephone to explain why she had to cancel the important appointment.

Linda's mother and her girlfriend contacted the Hermosa Beach police about the disturbing mystery. But neither of the women, or anyone they talked to, knew who the mysterious "Chuck" was or where Linda was planning to meet him after leaving her house Thursday morning. The concern and sense of dread increased during the weekend, and on Saturday Brooke and some other friends of Linda's began contacting local newspapers and television stations.

Linda was still missing on Sunday morning and when she didn't show up for worship services at the Baycities Community Church in adjacent Redondo Beach, the growing sense of dread increased. The model was seriously devoted to her Christian beliefs and was one of the most faithful members of the close-knit congregation. She would have attended the services if she could.

Her mysterious absence was baffling. She was always careful to make sure that at least one of her roommates knew her schedule for the day, where she was going to be and who she was going to be with. She updated her answering machine with calls as many times a day as was necessary in order to keep her circle of intimates aware of her schedule and whereabouts.

The busy model may have been charming and sweet, but she wasn't naive. She had been in the business long enough to know that certain dangers sometimes went along with the glamorous profession she had chosen for herself. She was also sufficiently successful so that she could turn down any assignment or photographer she wasn't comfortable with. All women have to use common sense precautions when dealing with strangers or casual associates and acquaintances, but the potential dangers are especially acute when the women are as attractive as Linda and her girlfriends in the business.

Girls who are smart and fortunate enough to make the right connections, are careful to work through reputable modeling agencies which help line up jobs and keep tabs on the backgrounds and reputations of photographers and clients who deal with them. Agents also make sure they know exactly when and where assignments are scheduled and who those assignments are with.

They also keep lists of photographers and anyone else in the business with shady reputations, and they share the information with other modeling and talent agencies. Photographers whose names appear on the blacklists quickly find it difficult to get assignments or to find models working with legitimate agencies who will pose for them.

The better agencies carefully screen new clients who contact them for models. If the agent doesn't know the customer, she checks with other agencies in the home city, then calls across the country to New York—or to Los Angeles—in order to cover the modeling centers on both coasts. If the client or photographer claims to be from Europe, the agent checks with colleagues there.

A good agent functions in some respects like a mother hen, or a protective big brother, looking out for the physical safety as well as the careers and financial welfare of their models. The ultimate responsibility, of course, rests with the models themselves. Making sure that others knew their whereabouts and refusing to put up with misbehavior by photographers, editors, or clients, are cardinal rules for women in the modeling trade. They know that if a photographer or client says or does something that makes them uncomfortable, it is better to walk out and call off the shoot rather than remain and take their chances.

Linda was aware of all those things, but Bettye Burgos, one of her roommates, worried that the disappearance was tied to the mysterious photo shoot. Bettye and another roommate, Kelly Flynn, also speculated that Linda may have been lured away for a bogus shoot by someone she met at one of the conventions she worked at as a model or hostess.

Even some of the most successful models sometimes agree to freelance an occasional shoot on the side without benefit of an agent, for a friend or someone else they have reason to trust. Some of Linda's friends suspected she knew the photographer or whoever the person was she went to meet, because she had to be sufficiently comfortable with that individual to go somewhere she wouldn't have access to a telephone. She may have worked with him before. That sounded reasonable, because despite her openness and loving nature, Linda wasn't easy to fool. She had heard all the lines about making her a big-time model or helping her break into movies, and she had a reputation for being able to spot a phony in an instant.

Anyone can buy a camera, have some business cards printed up, and put out a shingle. There are no diplomas to earn and display on office walls and no federal, state, or local regulatory agencies for photographers.

While having early-morning coffee with Bettye and talking over plans for the day, Linda hadn't said anything about a photo shoot or meeting with anyone named "Chuck." The only appointment she mentioned was the off-camera rehearsal and fitting at RML Productions in nearby San Pedro for the forties calendar shots.

She was a favorite with Roy Morales, the calendar producer. Roy, who is no relation to Brooke, was impressed with Linda's professional attitude and industriousness as well as with her beauty. She had posed for him before. Most recently she was photographed in a charming tiny white outfit including a pair of go-go boots and was scheduled to appear as "Miss November" for a 1996 pinup calendar called "Tantalizing Takeoffs."

Neither her longtime agent, Patty Brand, nor anyone else from the Brand Model Agency in Irvine, knew anything about the mysterious photo shoot. If Linda had gone on a job with a photographer, it wasn't set up by the agency.

Although Linda hadn't talked to her roommate or to Ms. Brand about a photo shoot on Thursday, she mentioned the job when she chatted by telephone around 8 A.M. with her boyfriend about meeting his flight at LAX and their plans for the weekend. They were looking forward to attending a barbecue Linda's parents were hosting at their home in Lakewood. Consequently, Bettye and others suspected the mysterious assignment was a last-minute development. It was clearly part of the puzzle. The model's roommates were also troubled because almost all her personal belongings were left behind. The only clothing missing was the clothes she wore and a few other items she apparently took with her as a possible change of costume for her work that day.

Unlike most men, women tend to notice particular elements of the wardrobes of their female friends, and one of Linda's roommates gave police a description of the missing items of clothing. A pair of fashionably funky Ugg boots was among the clothing missing from her closet. But most of her clothes, luggage, cosmetics, haircare products, even her toothbrush, were still in their proper place in her room.

The implications were distressing. No woman whose life and career were so firmly attached to her appearance would have deliberately gone off on a trip or for an extended period of time and left such vital personal accoutrements and grooming aids behind.

When Linda's worried fifty-seven-year-old mother contacted Hermosa Beach police and told them her daughter was missing, officers in the small oceanside resort town took the report seriously. Linda was an adult, free to go wherever she pleased, whenever she pleased without telling anyone. But she was also a clean living, considerate daughter and friend who would never have considered simply pulling a vanishing act.

Linda was surrounded by friends and family who cared deeply about her. Judging from all appearances she had a wonderful life. There were no pressures, no reasons in the world that any of her loved ones could think of that could possibly cause her to suddenly want to chuck it all and walk away. Her mysterious absence was sinister and singularly frightening. The longer she was missing, the more her family, friends, and law enforcement authorities feared she had met with foul play.

Most new law enforcement officers don't have to be in police work for very long before they learn not to take every report of a missing person at face value. Teenagers of both sexes run away every day, and most of the time they're back home in twenty-four hours or less.

Police department docket sheets are also filled with reports by fretful wives and husbands worried over missing spouses. Often there has been a quarrel or some other more longstanding domestic dustup, and after a few hours or a few days the missing spouse shows up at the front door, full of apologies and talking about giving the relationship another chance. Most missing persons cases handled by police in Hermosa Beach and in other jurisdictions around the country, resolve themselves within twenty-four hours. This was not to be the case with Linda Sobek.

The very last trace investigators were able to find of Linda ended after about ten o'clock Thursday morning when she was seen leaving Gold's Gym in nearby Redondo Beach following a workout. They were unable to find anyone who had seen her again.

On Monday morning, four days after her baffling disappearance, Hermosa Beach police announced to the press that Linda was officially listed as a missing person. By the time the announcement was made, Linda was already rapidly becoming the most famous citizen of the normally tranquil resort town that was home to roughly eighteen thousand residents packed into a miniscule area of 1.2 square miles along the south edge of Santa Monica Bay.

Police were initially a bit cryptic in public statements about the case. Detective David Rickey told a reporter that up to that time there was nothing to indicate foul play. He acknowledged he was treating the case as suspicious, however, because of the level of concern among her friends and their insistence that it was so unlike her to remain out of touch for so long. Officers with the small department had already been quietly investigating her disappearance. Linda's description and pertinent facts about the case were listed with other law enforcement agencies in California. A description of her car, including the license plate number, was also entered into a statewide police computer system. Court subpoenas were obtained for telephone records of calls made to and from Linda.

Within a short time three teams of investigators, a total of ten officers from the quiet town's thirty-five member police department, were working on the case. They followed up every possible lead to her whereabouts, no matter how weak it might seem to be.

Detectives talked with her boyfriend, with other chums and acquaintances, her roommates, and with members of her family. Police also began working on the twin tasks of trying to figure out who the photographer was and pinning down the location set up for the photo shoot. While continuing to press police to conduct a vigorous search, her friends swung into action on their own, seeking to find the missing woman or gather information to shed light on her disappearance.

They prepared flyers with one of her photos, a picture

of her 1992 Nissan, the license plate number, and a worded description of her appearance that offered a twenty thousand dollar reward for information leading to her return. The picture selected for Linda's flyer showed a woman dressed in a pair of ruggedly fashionable blue jeans, with a sleeveless top. A lustrous fall of near waist-length hair dropped casually over one shoulder while she leaned against a building block wall, with a thumb perfunctorily hooked into a pocket of the jeans. She was looking directly at the camera with her charming trademark smile. Linda's boyfriend and another pal put up the money for the flyers. Her friends were determined to do everything they could to find her, and just in case twenty thousand dollars wasn't enough to prime the information pump, they began raising more money in cash and pledges to add to the reward.

A newspaper reported that they also got up the money to hire private detective Anthony Pellicano to snoop around and see what information he could pick up about her whereabouts. Pellicano is no small-time sleuth. He's one of Tinseltown's most famous private investigators and has worked for such show business luminaries as Michael Jackson, Sylvester Stallone, and Roseanne. He was even called in by attorneys during the O. J. Simpson trial to do some work for the embattled retired LAPD detective, Mark Fuhrman.

Kelly Flynn's boyfriend, Paul Vreede, was a Tarzana businessman who printed and distributed listings for real estate companies, and he ran off fifty-three thousand copies of the flyers. Vreede stuffed most of them into packets alongside real estate listings he was mailing to coastal cities from Oxnard to San Diego. A few days later her friends gathered in Torrance to map out plans for wider distribution of the flyers.

Then her roommates, model chums, spouses, boyfriends, and girlfriends circulated throughout the Greater Los Angeles and South Bay areas distributing thousands more of the flyers. They passed them out at street corners, offered them to motorists, tacked them up on trees and on the walls of buildings, and posted them in the windows of retail stores, fast-food restaurants, and other business places.

Opening another front in the search, they talked wiith a psychic who advised them Linda's missing car was parked by a lamppost only five miles from her house.

Psychics can be helpful, and even police have begun to call on them for assistance in especially perplexing cases, but the data usually comes in bits and pieces and isn't always specific. Their information can be frustratingly vague and they often have difficulty exactly pinpointing dates, times, and locations. The mystics are likely to "see" bodies of water, mounds of earth, bridges, or certain types of buildings, and numbers that might be an age, or part of a date or address. The psychic Linda's friends consulted was unable to provide them with the exact location of her car.

By Sunday, the fourth day she was missing, friends were gathering together to exchange frightening theories about what might have happened to her. Some of the friendships went back to high school days. One of Linda's former school chums was Gail Spangler, and she was among the group of young people who met in Torrance to help distribute leaflets. The more people who knew about Linda, the better the chance was she would "come back," Ms. Spangler optimistically told a sympathetic news reporter.

As news of Linda's disappearance was passed by word of mouth, then picked up in the media and spread throughout the Los Angeles area, other friends began to contact her parents or her roomies at the big house in Hermosa Beach asking for additional information and offering help. There were lots of prayers at the Sobek home in Lakewood; at the rambling wood-frame, four-bedroom house in Hermosa Beach, and among the flock at Linda's church.

Every time the telephone rang, the hearts of her parents, brother, and other relatives who gathered in the cozy little home to share their strength and their fears, jumped. Usually it was another relative or someone else who knew and loved Linda, asking if there was any news. Often it was someone from the press.

Linda's mother did her part by talking with television, radio, and newspaper reporters about her missing daughter and the increasingly desperate search. Linda's description, and a description of her sporty little white Nissan and the number on her California license plate, ZZOL713, appeared repeatedly in broadcasts and in the print media.

The Sobeks kept their television set turned on and tuned to news shows almost nonstop throughout the early days of the ordeal. There was a lot of channel surfing. Whenever Linda's father caught a mention of the story, he whooped, "Here she is," and everyone headed for the set to listen for an update on the search.

Los Angeles television stations aired several shows about the missing beauty; the search was featured prominently on regular TV and radio news broadcasts; and daily and weekly newspapers throughout the Southland area carried regular stories. Then tabloid television shows including *Maury Povich*, *Leeza*, *Inside Edition*, and *Extra*, along with the Associated Press and other news wire services took the story national.

Linda was a classic beautiful blond California girl, just as Nicole Brown Simpson had once been, and there was even a professional football connection. She was a Raiderette who led cheers for the Los Angeles Raiders for five seasons until 1993, when she left by her own choice in order to devote more time to her flourishing modeling career. Several of her closest friends in the modeling world were current or former Raiderettes.

The massive publicity seemed to be working. On the Monday after Linda walked out of her house for the last time, Hermosa Beach police received more than one hundred tips. Most of the contacts were phoned in and ranged from people who believed they had seen Linda, her car, or suspicious characters who might have been involved in the disappearance, to concerned psychics.

Linda, or her car, or both, were reported as having been spotted in Southern California communities as varied as San Diego and San Bernardino. None of the tips led police to the missing model.

Then came the break. A community service worker assigned by the courts to a road cleanup crew, discovered a page from Linda's appointment book and some of her photographs in the Angeles National Forest. He was helping clear trash from an area along the Angeles Crest Highway above Altadena when he spotted a brown bag containing the pictures lying near a trash barrel. The photographs of a sexy model in various poses were typical of those Linda carried with her when she was interviewing for photo shoots.

The workman stumbled across the material on Saturday, two days after she dropped from sight. Then he gave the material to a National Park Service employee, who liked the pictures and kept them, along with the torn appointment book page. The park worker didn't recognize the importance of the find until Monday night when he saw pictures of the blond beauty broadcast on local television. Realizing the photos might provide a valuable clue to the whereabouts of the missing woman, he telephoned Hermosa Beach police that night. A short time later he told investigators his story and turned over the photos to them.

Tuesday morning HBPD detectives hurried to the turnout along the narrow highway to take a closer look and search for additional clues. A Dumpster holding trash collected by the work crew hadn't yet been hauled away from a central pickup site, and officers rummaging around inside collected additional pages torn from Linda's appointment book as well as snapshots of her parents and other family members.

Rags stained with a suspicious dark substance were

also found in the bag, but it couldn't be immediately determined if the smears were human blood. That job was turned over to technicians at the Sheriff's Department Crime Laboratory.

One of the pages from the calendar book was of special interest to the investigators. It was for Thursday, the day Linda disappeared. She had listed an appointment on the page for a meeting with someone from Hollywood at about 1 P.M.

Sergeant Paul Wolcott of the HBPD told reporters the find was "extremely valuable."

At an evening press conference police read a statement from Linda's family indicating they believed she somehow left the material at the turnout as a clue. They said they believed it was "a positive sign and that Linda is struggling to lead us to her whereabouts and to let us know that she is okay." The statement added, "Family and friends remain positive and continue their hope and prayers that she will be found safe and alive."

However, the rugged Angeles National Forest has a reputation as a sinister site for murder and a dumping ground for corpses. The new development was ominous.

The huge government preserve sprawls over 694,000 acres, roughly one thousand square miles. It is about the size of the entire state of Rhode Island and amounts to more than one-fourth of all the land in Los Angeles County. It is also only a few minutes away by car from the violent, drug-ridden streets of Compton, Watts, or South Central Los Angeles and from Hollywood's Sunset Strip with its pornography, pimps, prostitutes, and johns. The Angeles National Forest is a different world.

It was designated as a national forest in 1892 by President Benjamin Harrison, and is the second oldest in the country. It is also spectacularly beautiful, with areas usually defined by fluctuations in altitude where the steep ridges and valleys of the San Gabriel Mountains are spotted with enormous stands of big cone Douglas fir and canyon oak and other forests of Coulter pines or

mixed conifers. Desert areas and thickets of thorny chaparral are features of some of the lower ranges, particularly along the foothills and flatlands approaching the
east slopes.

Alongside the beauty, however, the preserve has seen
its share of violence. Love affairs gone awry have been
ended there among the silence of the darkly shadowed
woods with terrible and savage finality. Drug dealers and
other lawbreakers have permanently broken off professional relationships with former criminal colleagues
amid sudden blasts of gunfire. And rapists have lured or
transported victims to the sheltering darkness of the forest to be abused and murdered.

As convenient to the city and the clutter of suburbs
as it is, the forest is also used as a handy disposal area
for dumping the bodies of victims murdered elsewhere.
Some of the bodies are never found. Others are found
and never identified. Occasionally, human remains recovered from the forest are linked to some of the more
notorious criminals who have made major contributions
to the City of Angels' growing reputation for especially
infamous, bizarre, or gruesome crimes.

The remains of Cindy Lou Hudspeth, one of the
young women tortured, raped, and murdered by yet another pair of notorious Los Angeles area predators, killing cousins Angelo Buono and Kenneth Bianchi, were
recovered from the forest. The shocking series of sex
murders rumbled through the Los Angeles area in the
1970s and became known as the Hillside Strangler slayings because the victims were throttled and most of the
bodies were dumped in the hills. Cindy's corpse was
recovered after a pilot with the U.S. Forest Service
checking for fires spotted her Datsun near the bottom of
a steep hillside along the Angeles Crest where the high,
jagged, forested peaks separate the city and its near suburbs to the west from the parched and chaparral laced
desert lands to the east. The twenty-year-old waitress'
naked body, marked with what appeared to be knife cuts,

was stuffed inside the trunk. Her neck was deeply creased with the marks of a ligature.

Serial killer Randy Steven Kraft, who was arrested in 1983 when a California State Highway Patrolman stopped his erratically weaving car and found a dead Marine in the passenger seat, dumped at least one of his victims in the forest. The body of Rodger DeVaul was hidden in the rugged mountains a few weeks before his killer's arrest. Kraft was arrested, convicted of murdering sixteen young men over an·eleven-year-period, and sentenced to death for his orgy of torture, castration, and ghastly murder. A string of slayings of young men and boys which occurred in the Los Angeles area during Kraft's spree became collectively known as the Freeway Murders, and included several which were ultimately linked to other killers.

Joseph Gamsky, who is serving a life term in the notorious old California State Correctional Center at San Quentin for the murder of financial slickster Ron Levin, claimed the body was disposed of in an Angèles National Forest canyon. Levin's remains were never found. Gamsky, better known as Joe Hunt, is the former Beverly Hills based whiz kid who put together and headed an investment group of young Southern California·jet-setters who became notorious in the 1980s as the Billionaire Boys Club and were involved in big-time financial manipulations.

Seventeen-year-old Michelle Avila also wound up in the national forest after two of her teenage girlfriends accused her of sleeping with their boyfriends and drowned her. ''Missy's'' body was recovered in 1985 from under a log in a creek.

More recently, the headless corpse of convicted swindler Arthur Lee Evans was recovered from the forest. Evans was the owner of a brokerage firm that was once the largest in Orange County, Los Angeles County's nearest neighbor to the south.

Investigations of numerous other Los Angeles area

homicides have also turned to the dark forest as the result of confessions, information from tipsters, or the accidental discovery of remains. Hunters, hikers, picnickers, and Forest Service employes periodically stumble onto shallow graves, piles of bleached bones, and remains scattered by wild animals in the deep woods, canyons, and dry chaparral.

By the middle of November when the search for the former Raiderette turned to the Angeles, seven bodies had already been lifted from the forest floor that year.

Not all the predators that stalk the heavily forested mountains and precipitous canyon slopes are human, however. The national preserve is infested with rattlesnakes that roam the switchbacks, rocky mountainsides, and jagged canyons; mean-tempered western diamondbacks that can grow nearly seven feet long and as thick around the middle as a man's arm, and their slightly smaller cousins the more mildly dispositioned but superbly camouflaged red diamondbacks.

Citified picnickers, campers, hikers, fishermen, and other visitors who utilize the forest for recreation, as well as the occasional prospector who still pans or sets up sluices among the rocky creekbeds looking for gold soon learn to pay attention and look out when they hear the soft, dry rustle and click of the lumps of shed skin that form the snake's rattles at the base of the tail. Both species are capable of suddenly striking and critically injuring or causing death with the deadly poison injected by their sharp fangs.

At certain times of the year hunters are permitted into areas of the forest to track down and kill deer and smaller game. Protected herds of Nelson bighorn sheep also roam the craggy ridges of the higher elevations, where they are targeted by human poachers, anxious for trophies and meat. Coyotes are known to wander into residential areas along the lower slopes and attack pets and small children. There have been no recent accounts of bear attacks, but the bruins sometimes lumber through backyards in such nearby communities as Azusa, La Canada, and Monrovia. Cougars pose an even greater danger to humans. Less than a year before Linda's disappearance a bicyclist was pounced on and severely mauled by a mountain lion.

But the Angeles forest has other dangers for the careless, or hapless sojourner besides serial killers, sex slayers, hit men, and animal predators. And they're as modern as the drug trade that rages through the nation's second-largest city only a few miles to the east. Park rangers and sheriff's deputies ferret out from fifteen to twenty-nine marijuana plantations in the forest every year. At other times they pounce on manufacturers of methamphetamine, a powerful stimulant that is called by various names on the street including "meth," "speed," "crystal," "ice," or "crank." The Grub Street chemists drive into forest glades with pickup trucks and minivans outfitted with jerry-rigged laboratories to cook up their chemicals, where the odor and other giveaway clues are unlikely to attract the attention of neighbors or police. There is big money in the drug trade, and the pot farmers and unscrupulous chemists who use the forest are known for fiercely protecting their valuable products. Whenever the lawmen pounce on marijuana farmers or forest chemists, they usually find guns as well. Sheriff's deputies assigned to duty patrolling the forest are heavily armed with handguns and with AR-15 assault rifles.

It would seem that the forest, with all its beauty and grandeur, was no place for a beautiful model, unless she knew exactly where she was going and who she was going there with.

Yet, if Linda had somehow come to harm in the sprawling wilderness she wouldn't be the first stunning, blond, blue-eyed model who ended up there after mysteriously vanishing. On March 3, 1993, skeletal remains of twenty-year-old Kimberly Pandelios were discovered and retrieved from an isolated forest grave only three miles from where Linda's belongings were found more than two years later. And like Linda, when Kim was last heard from she was on her way to an apparent modeling assignment that cropped up at the last moment. A refugee from Communist Cuba, the winsome part-time model with the long frizzy Farrah Fawcett hairstyle that curled and flowed past her shoulders moved from Florida to California with her twenty-three-year-old husband, Peter, and year-old son, Nicholas, only four months before her disappearance.

The young family settled in Northridge and Kim busied herself with her duties as homemaker and new mother, but took time out when the opportunity arose for part-time modeling assignments. At about nine o'clock on Thursday morning, February 27, 1992, Kim left Nicholas with a baby-sitter while she drove to nearby Canoga Park where she was scheduled to undergo some job training with an insurance company. At noon she telephoned the sitter from a hairdressers to check on Nicholas and said she was going to meet a man named Paul, who had a connection with the modeling business. Kim explained they were planning a photo shoot and added she wouldn't be able to call from the site of the job because there wouldn't be a telephone available.

Paul telephoned Kim's house a bit later and asked where his model was. The sitter explained Kim was running late because she stopped to get her hair done. But Kim herself didn't telephone home again, and she didn't return to the house that night. Her young husband contacted just about everyone he could think of that night and the next day to ask about his missing wife, except police.

He waited until Saturday to notify authorities about her baffling disappearance because he believed that someone had to be gone for forty-eight hours before a missing person report could be filed. Years ago it was true that most police jurisdictions required twenty-four-or-forty-eight-hour waits before accepting missing persons reports, but the policies had changed. Like most other criminal investigations, in missing persons cases when foul play is a possibility, it is important for police to begin digging up information as soon as possible. The first twenty-four to forty-eight-hours after a crime can be critical to the investigation and information gathering process.

One of the most significant clues to Kim's disappearance developed the day after she dropped from sight. Her black 1991 Plymouth Laser was found abandoned and in flames on a remote stretch of the Angeles Forest Highway only about a mile and a half from the site where her skeletonized remains were eventually discovered.

Kim's husband and friends did the same thing Linda's chums did three years later. They got together and made their own efforts to dig up information about her whereabouts and what happened to her. They ran off thousands of flyers and posted them on utility poles, store windows, and on cars all over the San Fernando Valley.

Los Angeles police moved the case from their Missing Persons Bureau to Homicide, and one of their most experienced investigators, Philip Vannatter, was among eight detectives who checked out leads, asked questions, and began poking through telephone records. A few years later the crusty police veteran, generally referred to by colleagues as "Dutch," became known around the country as one of the lead detectives who investigated the Simpson case.

Authorities mustered a huge force of officers from the LAPD and Sheriff's Department to search the area around the mountain road where Kim's car was burned and gutted, and other parts of the wilderness for the missing woman or clues to her whereabouts. They included thirty eight recruits marshaled from the Police Academy, eight homicide detectives, four deputies from

Sheriff's Department Search and Rescue crews, and a helicopter with full crew.

Despite the spirited probe of the Pandelios disappearance, the baffling death of the petite stunner whose skull was discovered accidently by a gold prospector was never solved. Investigators never learned the identity of the mystery man she was planning to meet. Kim's brokenhearted husband moved back across the country to the Reading, Pennsylvania, area where his mother lived and began working to rebuild new lives for himself and his son.

Police still needed help from the public, such as the road worker's opportune discovery, if Linda's ominous vanishing wasn't to wind up the same way—as one of Southern California's frustrating unsolved mysteries. But by necessity police played it close to the vest and held back certain information.

The main focus of the investigation was clearly aimed at the national forest, especially on a narrow stretch of the two-lane Angeles Crest Highway near the turnout where Linda's daybook and photographs were found.

It is a rugged area at the three thousand-foot level. The rocky cliffs are sharp and steep, and deep ravines covered with brush and strewn with huge boulders plunge almost straight down.

U.S. Forest Service rangers and Los Angeles Sheriff's Deputies have grown accustomed to finding bodies, body parts, and skeletal remains of murder victims and suicides there. During some periods remains are discovered at the rate of one or two a week.

Earlier in the year the corpse of a seventy-six-year-old local man was bound on a stretcher and carried up a slope less than a half-dozen miles from the new search site by coroner's department officers and sheriff's deputies. The old man had been battered to death and wrapped in a sleeping bag before it was dumped. More recently, a few days before Linda disappeared, a human skull and some bone fragments from someone else who died in the forest or was transported there after death, was recovered near the new search area.

At about noon Tuesday a couple of hours after investigators in Manhattan Beach viewed the TV video, about twenty law enforcement officers and volunteers assembled near the turnout on the Angeles Crest Highway. The small man-made clearing in the forest located roughly between and to the east of Burbank and Pasadena was jammed with police and fire vehicles. Nearly two dozen media mobile units with crews were also there to record the event.

Members of the search team, including a few women, were telephoned or paged at their jobs and summoned for another of the frequent hunts through the rough terrain of the roadsides, ravines, and deeper areas of the forest and valleys. Sheriff's deputies who participate in the searches volunteer for the units they belong to. No one is drafted for the tough, sometimes dangerous task.

Although the official word to the waiting media indicated that the teams were looking for clues to Linda's disappearance, everyone knew they were searching for something they really hoped they wouldn't find: the model's body.

In the mountains, sheriff's reserve volunteers with search and rescue units based in Altadena, Montrose, and the Sierra Madre participated in the hunt, wearing heavy slacks and fire engine red shirts either with plastic helmets and goggles or blue caps. The special clothing was designed to make them easily visible, and to protect them from the rough terrain and such potential dangers as punctures or poison from the sharp chaparral, slashes from jagged rocks, and snakebite.

Members of the combined team held civilian jobs in professions ranging from high school teachers and driving instructors to sales reps and small business owners. One of the reserve officers worked at a day job teaching the rescue business to others. But members of the hastily assembled team were all veterans of other searches and

they went about their job with precision and professional
care. They spread out, positioning members about three
or four feet apart, then moved slowly and carefully
through the dry, tangled, red-tinged chaparral-covered
slopes of ravines with their eyes toward the ground, alert
for anything that might provide an additional clue to the
missing onetime cheerleader's whereabouts.

The bluff dropped off swiftly at about an 80 percent
grade, and although it wasn't steep enough to require
rappeling, it was a nasty place to search. The air was
hot and humid, and after only a few minutes work sweat
was clinging to armpits, staining shirts, and rolling off
foreheads. Despite all the public alarm and attention to
the destructive fires which regularly sweep through the
heavy forests that ring much of the Greater Los Angeles
sprawl on much of three sides, the search area hadn't
burned in forty years or more. Thickets of prickly brush,
poison oak, and sharp, jagged rocks were everywhere,
and some places were so nearly impassable that members of the combined search team got onto their hands
and knees or dropped onto their bellies, and crawled or
wriggled like the snakes that hunted there until they
reached clearer terrain. The rugged slope was meticulously inspected and as each area was gone over, it was
marked off with bright orange ribbon.

Nightfall comes early and rapidly in the national forest and the search teams were still going about their task
when the first faint hoots of owls and calls of other night
birds began drifting along the peaks and through the
ravines. The early evening shadows were already settling
over the area when the search was called off.

Not a single new clue to the former cheerleader's disappearance had been uncovered. Members of the search
and rescue units had given the job their best effort and
come up empty-handed. A pile of trash; useless scraps
of paper, crumpled-up beer cans, and an occasional
faded hat or other old piece of clothing that had nothing

to do with the missing model were all they had to show for their efforts. Police spokesmen announced that the area was scoured as thoroughly as possible, and the search teams would not be back the next day.

TWO

An Arrest

Ironically, it wasn't the official search teams combing the forest for traces of the missing model that came up with the next big break in the case. It was some of her friends.

Shawn Lucas, whose wife, Laurie, had been one of Linda's chums since they performed together with the Raiderettes, found the blond beauty's leopard-skin purse, makeup bag, hair curlers, a receipt from a printing and copy shop in Manhattan Beach, and some other articles. The cosmetic case was marked with Linda's initials, the curlers were marked with the letter "L," and the receipt was dated November 16—the date she disappeared. Lucas made the discovery while he and a group of friends were searching an area near the Clear Creek Ranger Station about three miles east of the location where the community service worker found the photographs and the daybook page.

It was the beginning of an eventful day for investigators and for Linda's family and friends; one that would be filled with drama and tragedy.

While Lucas and the others were combing the roadsides and nearby hills and gullies in the national forest, police were logging a report from an alert citizen who spotted Linda's car in the parking lot of a Denny's restaurant in Torrance a few minutes drive from her Hermosa Beach home. The tipster told officers he was driving through the lot and recognized the white sports coupe from descriptions on news accounts. The report, logged a few minutes after 1 P.M., was exactly the kind of break police were hoping for.

Discovery of the car near the rear of the parking lot fit in neatly with the notation on the Thursday page torn from Linda's daybook indicating she was scheduled to meet someone in the Los Angeles suburb. It also fit in with the psychic's vision. The lot was almost exactly five miles from Linda's home in Hermosa Beach, and the car was parked next to a light post near busy Crenshaw Boulevard. After talking with some of Linda's friends, investigators learned as well, that the popular eating spot was frequently used by models and photographers as a meeting place before shoots because of its easy access to U.S. Highway 405—the San Diego Freeway. The lot was within easy walking distance of the northbound on-ramp to the busy freeway, but there was no obvious damage to the car that might indicate it was left there after a fender-bender accident. There were no flat tires or indications of mechanical breakdowns. From all indications, the driver had chosen to leave the car there. The doors were locked and the sporty little Nissan was covered with a thin coating of dust, indicating it had sat in the same spot for days without being moved. An antitheft locking device was in place on the steering wheel.

Mary Dausner, manager of the restaurant in Torrance, which is inland and a few miles southwest of Hermosa Beach, told reporters that the car could have remained there unnoticed for a much longer time if it wasn't for the alert motorist. Cars come and go from the lot day and night, she pointed out, and the amount of time an individual vehicle is parked there isn't something that's normally noticed by anyone.

Seven minutes after the telephone report was logged in, officers from the Torrance Police Department arrived at the lot and sealed off the immediate area around the vehicle. Crime scene technicians and detectives were on the scene a few minutes later. The investigators made a careful search of the area looking for anything that might yield clues to the location of the owner or to anything else of value. The only item of possible interest found outside the vehicle was a partially filled garbage bag lying nearby. It was carefully collected and tagged with a note indicating the location it was picked up and the time. During later inspection it was determined the garbage bag and its contents had no connection with the missing woman.

While the search team worked, patrons entering and leaving the restaurant peered curiously at the small knot of police officers. Occasionally someone peeked through the window of the restaurant toward the men in the parking lot, apparently unaware that the intriguing flurry of activity was tied to the search for the missing model that was so prominently featured in recent news reports.

At last the Nissan was loaded onto the flatbed of a tow truck and hauled a few miles east to the Sheriff's Department Crime Laboratory in the town of Carson. Torrance Police Department motorcycle officers escorted the vehicles to the neighboring community.

Before the flatbed even arrived to haul the car to the crime lab, other officers were already meeting with LA County Assistant DA's to prepare search warrants so the vehicle could be checked for clues. A short time later, after the warrant was issued, a team of detectives and forensic technicians carried out a meticulous search. Everything inside the little sports coupe was removed, painstakingly recorded on a list and tagged with a word or two of physical description, the exact location it was found, and the time it was logged as evidence. The glove compartment was emptied of every item. Then the trunk was emptied and everything inside was added to the neatly kept log. A white plastic bag, envelopes, and a map book were among the articles removed from the car.

Forensic technicians also swept and vacuumed the interior, looking for trace evidence that could be as minute and furtively elusive as a piece of lint, a paint chip, thread, a single hair, or a spot of blood. Later, inside the crime laboratory, technicians emptied the bag and carefully examined the contents. The examination was first conducted with the naked eye, then after selecting specific elements for closer attention, by microscope. Somewhere down the road, the work of the technicians, chemists, and other forensic scientists could become vitally important in criminal or civil proceedings. More immediately, their findings might provide important clues to investigators who were still working to locate the missing model and to determine exactly what happened to her.

The technicians worked with extreme care. Embarrassing memories of the recently concluded O. J. Simpson trial debacle were still fresh in the minds of police and their colleagues in other branches of the local criminal justice system. No one wanted to chance a repeat of the fierce criticism and public humiliations that accompanied the earlier proceeding, occurring at some point down the line in the Sobek case.

But the disappearance was already attracting widespread national attention, and the pace of the investigation was rapidly picking up. Hermosa Beach police called for assistance from Los Angeles County Sheriff Sherman Block. An offer of help was also accepted from the resident agent at the Redondo Beach office of the FBI to help locate possible witnesses outside the California area.

Hermosa Beach is a normally quiet seaside town of about twenty thousand people, with a small police force. By contrast, with a complement of eight thousand uniform officers and three thousand civilians, Los Angeles County supports the largest sheriff's department in the nation. The sheriff oversees the employment of more people than the total population of many cities and towns. Importantly, the department also has access to teams of highly trained veteran homicide investigators, laboratory technicians, and other forensics experts. The resources in manpower and physical facilities and capabilities are far greater than those of any single suburban community in the county.

Formal entry of the sheriff into the case also promised to ease problems tied to jurisdictional matters in the burgeoning investigation. The City of Angels is surrounded by an organized scatter of municipalities spread out among the hills, valleys, and flat basin land of the coastal area. Each of the suburban communities have their own police departments which patrol and jealously keep the peace in their own particular patch of the solid urban sprawl that radiates out from the nation's second largest city until it is stopped by mountains, dense forest, or the Pacific Ocean. A countywide agency such as the Sheriff's Department could most easily avoid the sort of disputes that often develop between police officers in different municipalities. Los Angeles County Sheriff's officers were in the best position to bring about the kind of smooth cooperation and sharing of information and resources necessary to an investigation that had already expanded into several separate jurisdictions.

With the agreement of their colleagues in Hermosa Beach, sheriff's investigators took over the lead role in the joint operation. Before many more days elapsed, several additional local law enforcement agencies and others across the country would be drawn into the probe.

As the Sheriff's Department added its considerable investigative resources to the case, a team of homicide detectives drove to the Los Angeles International Airport (LAX) and picked up a thirty-five-year-old Los Angeles man. Morgan Carey voluntarily accompanied police to the Lennox Station to be questioned. After about an hour he was released and permitted to board a flight for New

York. Carey was not considered to be a suspect in the disappearance, police said.

While Carey was resuming his interrupted trip, homicide investigators were busy on another more promising front. At the request of Hermosa Beach police, sheriff's deputies took up a post outside a large, two-story woodframe house at 1937 Canyon Drive in Hollywood. The name of the occupant, the telephone number, and the address, only a few blocks from neighboring Griffith Park, were discovered when police searched the forest Dumpster. The information was on a document for the loan of a 1996 Lexus 450 LX from the manufacturer's fleet which they found while they were leafing through the torn out schedule book pages. The forty thousand dollar vehicle owned by the Toyota Motor Company was checked out on the same day Linda vanished. At last police had the name of a man who was believed to have met with Linda on the day she disappeared.

At 7:45 Tuesday morning HBPD Detective Raul Saldana telephoned Charles Edgar Rathbun at his blue-and-white painted house in Hollywood and asked about the loan agreement paper found among Linda's personal possessions alongside the forest highway.

Rathbun explained that he was a photographer and picked up the prototype sports utility vehicle from a company lot on 190th Street in Torrance at about 9:30 Thursday morning so he could shoot pictures of it for an automotive magazine. The photographer said he called Linda from a car phone after picking up the Lexus, to "touch bases," and arranged to meet her at the nearby Denny's at 11 A.M. They met in the restaurant parking lot for about fifteen-to-twenty minutes and he looked over her portfolio but she was too "hardlooking" to use for the photo shoot, Rathbun told the detective. When they parted, she was alive and well, he claimed.

Saldana asked Rathbun when he was most recently in

the Angeles National Forest. The photographer replied that it had been three weeks.

After asking him to come to the HBPD headquarters later in the day for a more complete interview, the homicide detective temporarily suspended the conversation. Rathbun agreed to meet with him at 11 A.M., but Saldana played it safe. He arranged for the sheriff's deputies to keep an eye on the photographer. If Rathbun left the house, it was important that he be followed and his movements kept track of. Saldana and his colleagues were rapidly developing information to back up growing suspicions that the freelance photographer was closely tied to the model's disappearance.

Investigators who fanned out to interview employees and regular customers at Denny's also located a witness who recalled seeing a pretty blond woman climbing into a snazzy sports utility vehicle that was driven away by the photographer late Thursday morning, the day Linda disappeared. The witness remembered also that she was wearing curlers in her yellow hair.

It seemed highly probable that investigators had identified the mysterious "Chuck," that Linda told Mrs. Sobek she was going to meet, during the last hurried telephone chat between mother and daughter. Locating a witness who could place the photographer in a car with the model was one more encouraging development in a case that appeared to be suddenly shaping up.

Just as the earlier discovery of the photos and page from the appointment book had done, the newest revelations added to the discomfort and sense of foreboding over the missing model's fate. Lucas's discovery occurred in the same general area as the earlier material, only a short distance from where the remains of Kimberly Pandelios were recovered. But the puzzles over the fate of the two models were being linked by other factors.

Both women were reportedly on their way to meet a mystery man when they vanished. Linda indicated she was going to meet a man she knew as "Chuck." Kim was going to meet a man she knew as "Paul," at his studio in the Burbank-Glendale area. She had talked to him for some time about getting into modeling on a regular basis instead of the hit and miss shoots she was currently accepting. And she had once had a meeting with him at a Denny's restaurant. Kim's husband told police the man named "Paul" telephoned on Thursday night, after she vanished, and said she had visited with him and forgotten her appointment book. Police weren't able to trace the caller or to come up with a full identification for "Paul." But a hiker stumbled onto Kim's address book along an embankment near a forest campground and turned it over to police after seeing a news report about the missing woman. Most of the pages were ripped out. Discovery of Kim's mutilated address book later formed an intriguing parallel with developments in the search for Linda. The similarities weren't lost on the steadily growing body of police officers looking for the Hermosa Beach model.

Rathbun didn't show up at the HBPD. He was already late when he telephoned Saldana a few minutes before noon and said he was running behind schedule and would be at the station in about an hour.

"I guess you're anxious to talk to me," the detective later recalled him saying.

"I'm anxious to talk to anyone who's had contact with Miss Sobek," Saldana replied.

"Well, I guess you're anxious to talk to me because I was the last one to see her," Rathbun continued. He was correct about that, but even though it was true that he telephoned a client about some pictures, his failure to keep his promise to meet with Saldana at 11 A.M. wasn't totally due to a need to wrap up a few business matters.

While the detective and his colleagues waited for Rathbun at the police station, the photographer was thinking about ending it all, telephoning friends and business associates, and getting roaring drunk. He telephoned a Glendale woman he had dated after meeting her on her job in Los Angeles at the Petersen Publishing Company, one of his major clients. He talked with some people from *Truckin* magazine at the McMullin Argus Publishing Company, another important client with headquarters in suburban Placentia. And he telephoned a friend, then sent her a rambling suicidal message on his fax machine, pleading that he wanted God to forgive him because he killed someone and couldn't live with that knowledge.

The friend was Shannon Christine Meyer, a thirty-seven-year-old woman he had dated one time. She was also a reserve deputy sheriff, who graduated from the police academy the previous February and was assigned to the Temple City Sheriff's Horse Station.

"Do you know about the disappearance of that model, Linda Sobek?" he asked during the phone call.

When Deputy Meyer replied she didn't know anything about the model, Rathbun proceeded to tell her he accidently struck her with a Lexus then abandoned her body after she died. "I was shocked," the deputy recalled in later courtroom testimony about the conversation.

The rookie cop was sufficiently shaken immediately after her talk with Rathbun to telephone civil attorney James D. Nichols and blurt out a bare bones version of what was going on. The lawyer was a partner in the law firm, Bonne, Bridges, Mueller, O'Keefe and Nichols, with offices on Wilshire Boulevard in Los Angeles, and specialized in medical malpractice defense. Criminal law wasn't his area of expertise. But a man appeared to be on the verge of suicide, and there was no time to waste. Nichols and Meyer hurried to the house on Canyon Drive in Hollywood. It was about four o'clock Wednesday afternoon when they parked in front of the house. They were met moments later by Rathbun, who emerged carrying a semiautomatic .45-caliber pistol. He was crybaby drunk, reeked of vomit, and his light wool jacket and white shirt were smeared with ugly stains. He had barely lurched out of the house to confront the man and woman when the pistol discharged.

The single bullet ricocheted, and a chunk of shrapnel slashed into the left arm of the sheriff's deputy. Residents of the normally quiet neighborhood later recalled watching in wide-eyed wonder while the woman in the "USA" sweatshirt shrieked and clutched at her bloody arm. They said she was running and screaming for someone to dial 911. Their disheveled neighbor meanwhile stood weaving at the front of the house with a pistol in his hand, looking stunned and confused.

Nichols, the other participant in the drama, was faced with an armed drunk who had just fired one shot from a pistol; and with an injured woman who appeared to be skating on the verge of hysteria.

As calmly as he could, Nichols coaxed Rathbun to put the gun down, while urging the injured sheriff's deputy, "Keep it quiet. Calm down, calm down." His efforts worked. Meyer calmed down, and the gunman released the weapon. Still being careful not to alarm the distraught drunk, Nichols scooped up the .45. He removed the ammunition clip and put it in his coat pocket, then stuck the pistol in the waistband of his pants in order to keep it away from the owner. Rathbun stumbled unsteadily back inside the house, followed by the lawyer.

It wasn't a typical afternoon in the comfortable, normally quiet neighborhood of well-kept homes and tree-lined streets at the base of the Hollywood Hills. Residents were even more surprised when they learned that the uncommon ruckus was related to the highly publicized search for the missing model from Hermosa Beach that had dominated local TV newscasts during the last few days.

The excitement wasn't over yet. The team of sheriff's deputies watching the house moved in and were joined almost immediately by a team of officers from the HBPD who were already driving on their way there when the violent drama began to unfold. Officers from the LAPD Hollywood Division Station also converged on the house, and the 1900 block of Canyon Drive quickly filled with uniformed and plainclothes officers and patrol cars with crackling radios and flashing overhead light bars.

As far as police were concerned when they arrived at the home, they were confronted with a still volatile situation. Some people were inside; at least one of them was armed; and another person had already been shot. It was difficult to immediately determine if anyone inside the house was being held against their will as hostages.

Uniform officers were quickly posted around the house to keep neighbors and anyone else who was not there on law enforcement business away from the danger zone. Then an LAPD officer telephoned the house to advise Rathbun to walk outside with his hands in the air.

Nichols answered the phone and identified himself. He said Rathbun was with him, and they knew police were outside. Rathbun was ready to give himself up without causing any further problems. The lawyer added that the distraught man had been drinking and said the two of them would walk outside together. In response to the policeman's suggestion, Nichols described the clothing each of them was wearing. The lawyer was dressed in a tan jacket and blue jeans, and Rathbun had on a dark colored light wool jacket with blue Levi's. Rathbun was no longer armed, Nichols added. Then he turned the telephone over to his client.

Rathbun listened while the policeman identified himself and ordered him to walk through the front door with his hands up. The policeman stressed that it was important to immediately follow every command of the officers waiting outside the house. Rathbun agreed and hung up the telephone.

While police crouched behind cars with their weapons trained on the front door, the photographer and the lawyer walked out of the house with their hands in the air. A rush of police in uniform and in plain clothes converged on the two men. The law officers made a rapid search of their clothes, then clamped handcuffs around their wrists. One officer pulled the pistol from Nichols's waistband, and with the muzzle pointed to the ground quickly checked the chamber for bullets. Nichols was already explaining that he was Rathbun's lawyer, and trying to bring the lawmen up-to-date on what had been going on as his arms were being pulled behind his back.

While the handcuffed men stood against a block wall near the house for a few moments, Nichols repeated some last-minute advice to his client not to talk to anyone or sign anything outside the presence of an attorney. He also repeated the warning to some of the officers. He didn't want anyone interrogating his client unless a lawyer was present. As Rathbun and Nichols were surrounded by stern-faced police officers, a team of Emergency Medical Technicians (EMTs) from the Los Angeles Fire Department administered first aid to Deputy Meyer. Then she was transported to the Hollywood station of the LAPD on North Wilcox Avenue. The tiny chunk of shrapnel barely grazed her arm, and the injury was more painful and frightening than serious.

The two men, each surrounded by cordons of officers, were hustled into the backseats of separate police cars a few moments later. When the lawyer settled back against the hard plastic seat, it put pressure on his cuffed hands, and he complained that his circulation was being cut off and he was in pain. One of the officers loosened the cuff on his right hand. Nichols sat in the car with his hands cuffed behind him for an hour or more, unaware of what was going on with his client. Then he was moved to another car, with a soft seat, and driven to the LAPD Hollywood Station.

Inside the station he was ordered to empty his pockets, his personal property was inventoried, and he was led into a holding cell. Nichols was apparently being held under suspicion of carrying a concealed weapon—the empty pistol he stuck in his waistband.

Deputy Meyer was also led to a room by herself to await the arrival of investigators, who were anxious to hear her story. A bit later, homicide investigators listened incredulously while the freshman cop told them Rathbun confessed to her that he was involved in the death of the missing model. Deputy Meyer said she didn't pass the information on to her colleagues or superiors because she didn't believe the story. Her friend had a reputation as a practical joker, she explained. The deputy repeated the story of her telephone conversation with Rathbun. She said the photographer told her he hired Linda for a photography shoot and accidentally hit her with the vehicle.

While the reserve deputy was being grilled by fellow officers and the civil lawyer was getting his first inside look at the down-and-dirty workings of law enforcement and the criminal justice system, Nichols's client was perching miserably on a hard bunk bed. When Rathbun first arrived at the Hollywood station, he was treated much like his lawyer. His pockets were emptied, his wristwatch was taken away, and after an inventory form was filled out he was led to a holding cell. Unlike the lawyer, Rathbun was booked for investigation of murder. He was still handcuffed when he was locked inside the cell, but he wasn't left alone very long.

Saldana and Sheriff's Detective Mary Bice, who were leading the homicide investigation, converged on the station along with several other officers from the HBPD and the Sheriff's Department.

Before their arrival, Detective Michael McDonagh, of the LAPD Hollywood Division's Homicide Unit, visited the prisoner in the holding cell and removed his handcuffs. McDonagh asked Rathbun if he needed to use a bathroom or wanted anything to drink, and the dejected prisoner answered negatively to both questions. As he prepared to leave, McDonagh explained he wasn't involved in the case but that other investigators from the Sheriff's Department and the HBPD were on their way to the station.

"Yeah, I figured they would be coming," Rathbun responded.

McDonagh left Rathbun to himself and walked two cells down the corridor to another cubicle where Nichols was waiting, also in handcuffs. The detective introduced himself, removed the manacles, and told the lawyer basically the same thing he told Rathbun.

Nichols explained to the homicide detective that he was a lawyer and said he and Deputy Meyer went to Rathbun's house because they were concerned the photographer was suicidal. Nichols said he saw Rathbun fire the pistol that led to the deputy's injury but described the shooting as totally accidental.

McDonagh led the lawyer out of the cell and ushered him into the detective squad room, then into an interview room where he poured him a cup of hot coffee to sip. After making sure the lawyer was settled in, McDonagh returned to the detectives squad room and met briefly with Saldana and Bice to bring them up-to-date on the status of Nichols and Rathbun.

Then he returned to Rathbun's cell and led the lanky, towheaded suspect outside and through the front lobby of the police station to another interrogation room. The officer directed Rathbun to sit on a straightback chair pulled up to a plain wood table. McDonagh advised the suspect that some detectives would be there in a few minutes to talk with him, then turned and left the room. He locked the door of the windowless cubicle behind him. Finally, as previously agreed with Saldana and Bice, McDonagh got an audio cassette tape and placed it in a recorder in the station's sound room, then turned it on so the interview could be taped.

When Saldana and Bice at last walked into the spartanly furnished room where the dejected prisoner was waiting, his eyes were bloodshot, his jacket was splattered with his own vomit, and the stink of stale booze hung heavily in the air. The photographer looked like hell warmed over, but he remembered Nichols's advice.

The two detectives had barely entered the room, fussed briefly about the heat inside, and introduced themselves before Rathbun told them he had been advised not to talk unless he had an attorney with him.

It wasn't an especially auspicious beginning for an interrogation, but the detectives wanted to salvage what they could from the opportunity. They desperately needed to know where the missing woman was. If there was any longer any hope that she might still be alive, the prospect appeared to be about as faint as the chances the two experienced detectives would open the talk by offering their prisoner a cold Budweiser. But they had to find out for themselves and make sure she was beyond help.

"Uh-hum, okay," Saldana muttered, in response to the nervous outburst. "I . . . I realize that, okay?" Then he pressed on. Saldana explained they weren't there to question him about how Linda died but merely wanted to find the girl.

"And the reason we're in here talking now is, if anything, what we wanted to do is—there's a lot of people who really care about this gal, okay? And we'd like to make them feel better, make them feel whole, okay?"

"Um-huh," Rathbun agreed.

Saldana explained they were talking about getting the woman back. "We're in here, talking about that, you know? She would be given back to her mom and dad and friends and such." He asked the dejected man if he would be willing to help return the woman to her family.

"I wish I could. I just want to remember what, uh,

what I did after, uh . . . after the accident, so . . ."

Up to that time in the interview, no one had said anything about an accident, and the statement was the kind of remark that no interrogator could allow to simply slide by without expansion.

"After the accident?" the detective asked.

"Uh-hum."

"I don't . . . I don't understand," Saldana responded. "You had an accident?"

Rathbun wasn't ready to be drawn into a detailed discussion of the matter.

"Again, you're—you shouldn't talk to me about—about what went on, you know? I've been advised not to talk about it all, so," he stammered.

The investigators were up to their shoulder holsters in a perilously dicey situation.

They sincerely wanted to locate the missing model, but they couldn't do that without more facts. Although the old-time third degree depicted in grainy black-and-white movies is no longer allowed during interrogations, police are still permitted to stretch the truth—even lie when they're engaged in the critical business of trying to squeeze information out of a suspect. Direct force and intimidation is strictly off-limits, but there are other ways for a skillful interrogator to break down defenses and dig out the details they want. Nevertheless, some of the techniques used by successful interrogators aren't very nice. They can be sneaky or mean and can sometimes come extremely close to straying over the line of what's legally permissible or otherwise acceptable to the courts.

It seemed that Saldana and Bice weren't even skating on thin ice but were plunging straight through the surface and rapidly sinking into the mud at the bottom.

The Fifth Amendment to the U.S. Constitution is an integral element of the Bill of Rights and guarantees protection against self-incrimination. It makes it clear that suspects in criminal cases have the right to counsel.

Those rights were upheld by the U.S. Supreme Court and were refined in rulings requiring that defendants be read the so-called Miranda warning at the beginning of any interrogation.

The warnings, named after Ernesto Miranda, a kidnap-rapist from Phoenix who was imprisoned in Arizona, basically advises suspects before questioning that they have a Constitutional right to refuse to talk, that any statements they make can be used against them, they have a right to remain silent until they have an attorney present, and if they can't afford to pay a lawyer the state will provide one for them. The 1966 Supreme Court Miranda ruling specifically states that as soon as a suspect requests a lawyer, police must stop the interrogation until an attorney has been provided. Since that time, the controversial warning created by a slim five-to-four margin of a high court dominated by liberal Chief Justice Earl Warren has become a staple of police work and of television and movie drama.

The convict who started all the fuss was retried without his confession, found guilty once more, and returned to prison. He was eventually released and spent most of his waking hours hanging out in bars in and around Phoenix where he drank and boasted about his history-making feat. He carried business cards identifying himself as the famous Miranda the warning was named after, and sometimes managed to swap one of them with another barfly for a free drink. In 1976 the boozy local celebrity was stabbed to death in a barroom scuffle.

Even though Miranda, the man, died the Supreme Court ruling named after him lived on, and failure of police to properly repeat the warnings recited in the name of the departed rapist have led to a number of failed prosecutions or reversals of convictions. Like it or not, criminal investigators can't afford to ignore Miranda. It must be scrupulously observed at interrogations, and ideally police recite the five points of Miranda aloud, then have the suspect read a form listing the warning and waiving his (or her) rights under the Fifth Amendment.

Getting their job done while complying with the warning, which some people in the criminal justice season refer to as "famous" and others as "infamous," can present investigators with a fine line to walk. It can be extremely difficult to find a balance between the necessity to protect the public by bringing to justice criminals who rape, rob, and murder, while complying with the stern demands of the courts to protect the constitutional rights of suspects.

To many law-abiding citizens, it seems as if high court decisions on both the state and federal levels have stacked the deck so solidly against police and prosecutors in favor of rapists, child molesters, stick-up artists, and serial killers that obtaining confessions in this day and age is a virtual impossibility. The bad guys don't observe anyone's rules except their own, but the protectors of the public are expected to behave with Marquis of Queensberry courtesy and consideration. Nevertheless, criminal confessions are obtained by skillful police officers every day. Usually it's done by the use of common sense, and normal powers of persuasion. Obtaining a good statement that will stand up in court is an art that for many veteran investigators is part intuition, part seat-of-the-pants experience, and part classroom imparted skills. But one of the most important things for any criminal investigator to remember while conducting an interrogation is when to back off.

Detectives Saldana and Bice were only a few minutes into their inteview before Rathbun had twice asked in very clear terms for a lawyer. The requests were side-stepped. Eventually, he repeated the request ten more times, but each time he asked, either Saldana or Bice danced away from the subject and continued their questioning.

There were other questionable elements about the less-than-perfect proceeding as well, that opened the possibility of serious problems for police and prosecutors somewhere down the line.

No one read the suspect his Miranda rights. The two detectives and the morose photographer sat across from each other in the little room sparring for more than an hour, and apparently there was no mention from anyone of the warning.

Outside the police station, even though the sunny Southern California day was rapidly waning, temperatures were still warm. Inside the cramped, enclosed room it was uncomfortably hot and stuffy. Something was wrong with the thermostat, and officers were unsuccessful in earlier efforts to turn it down. Rathbun had also done a prodigious amount of boozing earlier in the day and he asked to use the toilet, but the detectives had important matters they wanted to work through first. They held him off, even though he asked several times, and moved on with the questioning.

Dropping the matter of an accident for the time being, investigator Bice asked the suspect if he had brothers and sisters. Rathbun said he had a brother and two sisters. They were all older than he was.

The photographer also said he knew what they were getting at with the reference to family. "Linda was a friend of mine," he blurted out. "She really was."

Saldana assured him that they realized that, and they didn't think he was a bad person. "We thought if you're a bad guy, you wouldn't've tried to get help. You wouldn't've tried to . . . tried to tell somebody, okay?" Rathbun had told them he tried to find help after striking the model with the car.

Now he said he couldn't even remember where he left the girl. He talked of the accident, of never seeing anyone die before, and of never hurting anyone or anything. "I've never killed anything in my life," he declared.

Detective Bice asked where they were when Linda was struck. Rathbun said they were at the El Mirage dry lake bed, adding that the location on the Mojave Desert near the town of Palmdale was a spot he had used as a backdrop for some of his photographs in the past. "You get beautiful light out there. You get . . . you get beautiful plumes off of the back of the cars . . ."

Rathbun specialized in photographing new cars and trucks, often with eye-catching young females as props, and frequently set up shoots on the desert and in the forest preserve. According to his account, he and the model drove across the mountains together in the new gleaming white utility vehicle, tooling along the Angeles Crest Highway until they reached the dry lake.

Continuing to respond to questions by Bice, Rathbun said it was near sunset when he and Linda were working at El Mirage. His enthusiasm for his work was obvious, and Bice moved in to take advantage of the opportunity to develop a temporary bond with the suspect by indicating personal interest in the profession. She agreed that sunset was a good time to take pictures and mentioned a conversation she had with another photographer about the use of natural light and shadows in a photo shoot. Throughout the brief exchange she was careful to keep the focus of the banter on the location where the reputed accident occurred.

"That's a long way out," she said of the lake bed. "I can see why you wouldn't remember."

Rathbun replied that it was a ninety-minute drive, and he couldn't recall some details because he "freaked out," after the mishap.

"You don't remember when you came back because you were freaked out?" Bice asked.

"I was just numb."

"And scared?" Saldana added. The detective's tone was wondering, sympathetic, as if he could imagine himself in the same position of suffering such awful emotional trauma and sudden panic.

"Yeah, I was very scared."

The interrogation was a time-consuming and tedious process. At times they moved back and forth over information previously covered, occasionally refining a description or picking up a new detail. In the meantime, bit by tortured bit, the photographer was relating a tragic story to the two detectives he was closeted with.

According to his account, Linda was struck with the spinning 1996 Lexus while he was showing her how to perform a high-speed 360-degree driving and spinning maneuver that people in the trade refer to as "doughnuts." Speaking haltingly, and choking up at times, the photographer said he took some action shots of Linda driving the prototype sports utility vehicle. They started snapping pictures about 3:30 P.M., and after a while they moved to a large dirt basin a short distance west of the lake bed just off one of the access roads to El Mirage. The afternoon was rapidly waning away but the light was still good.

Rathbun wanted her to perform the "doughnuts," but she didn't know how. So she climbed out to watch while he revved up the engine of the shiny new Lexus, roared in her direction, then twisted the wheel sharply and pressed the brake so that the rear end spun around in tight circles. But he lost control of the rapidly spinning four thousand-pound vehicle and the rear end slammed into Linda while she stood nearby watching the stunt. Rathbun said he heard a "thud" and leaped from the vehicle, rushing to the stricken girl. She was sprawled motionless on the ground apparently unconscious.

Rathbun at first said he left her in the middle of the desert. A bit later, he changed his story and told the detectives that after he was unable to revive her he swept her into his arms, loaded her into the car, and started driving. He was cradling her head in his hands, but she couldn't breathe. Rathbun said he was racing along the mountain road toward the Antelope Valley below to find medical help for the critically injured model when he realized it was too late. She was dead.

The grim-faced homicide detectives listened and watched, while the rumpled man forced the words out through tears and moans. Continuing his story, the photographer said he panicked and decided to get rid of the corpse. He drove around aimlessly for two or three hours, until darkness descended on the forest. Somewhere along the rugged trail he turned off on a narrow side road and at last skidded the vehicle to a stop, climbed out and scooped out a shallow trench in a flat area of sand and gravel. Then he dropped the limp body of the young woman inside. After scattering a thin covering of dirt over the corpse, he drove back to the city, getting rid of her belongings along the way. Finally, he returned the Lexus to the manufacturer's fleet, picked up his own car, and drove back to his home.

Detective Bice later stated in court documents that even though Rathbun told them he killed the model, she believed there was a chance Linda might still be alive and possibly in need of medical help. The detective said she considered it imperative to find the woman as soon as possible.

Saldana filed a similar declaration. ''My sole purpose in questioning Mr. Rathbun was to locate Linda Sobek so that if she was still alive but injured, she could be given immediate medical attention,'' he stated. ''Although Mr. Rathbun maintained during our conversation that he had accidentally killed Linda Sobek, I did not feel that Mr. Rathbun had the medical training to know for sure whether or not Linda Sobek was dead or alive.'' Saldana added that although he verbally agreed with the suspect at times during the interrogation that the model was dead, ''I only did this to enlist Mr. Rathbun's cooperation in helping us find Linda Sobek.''

The statements held important ramifications that would be fought out in a courtroom at the proper time and were linked to a legal doctrine that gives police more leeway during interrogations when someone's life might be saved by quick action or attention.

Continuing the interrogation, the detectives suggested possible routes Rathbun might have taken to and from the lake bed, struggling to pin down exact locations and other important details. He responded as if he wanted to help, but he had trouble with the exact names of highways and roads. He knew how to drive to the lake bed, but he didn't know all the details about road names and highway numbers.

Bice asked how much dirt he spread over Linda's desert grave. "I don't know. I felt like I committed murder," he replied.

"Uhhhm," Saldana murmured. It was a response that acknowledged the remark but was safely noncommital. The detective asked the suspect if he used his hands to scoop the dirt over Linda. Rathbun said he did, and a bit later in response to questions by Bice, added that he found a board and used it as a shovel.

"You know, I come from that area, and, uh, at night it gets real cold," Bice observed.

"Yeah, it does," Rathbun agreed.

"And the dogs, and the, uhm, other animals like coyotes, and uhm, even bobcats, and uhm . . ."

Rathbun knew where Bice was heading with her remarks about nocturnal desert fauna. The ghastly mental image of the body of the dead girl lying under a thin film of dirt and pebbles where it was prey to animal predators and scavengers hung heavy in the air of the uncomfortably hot interrogation room.

The photographer said he wished he could help the officers find Linda, but he didn't remember where he left the body. When he left the lake bed he began driving down the road and didn't know where he turned off, or where he went. He just drove. Furthermore, it was dark.

"Like she said, unfortunately, what, what's gonna' happen is, is somebody is gonna' stumble upon—probably quite a few different locations Linda will be located by the time these critters end up, uh—" Saldana was back on the subject of the girl's defenseless corpse and desert predators, but he was having trouble blurting out what he wanted to say. So Bice interjected herself into the tortured monologue and finished the ghoulish thought.

"You know they're going to take—they're going to pull what clothes she had on, off. They're going to, they're going to take her hands and, you know, chew on her face, the ants and other things—and she was a beautiful girl. It's just not fair to do that to her family. Do you know what that's going to be like to put into a box, so you can put it in the ground. I, uh, just can't imagine doing that to one of my kids. She was a beautiful girl."

The dreadful mental vision of insects, worms, or possum, racoons, and other scavengers tearing at the tender body of the lovely model was back again, and it wouldn't be the last time it was recalled.

Rathbun's cheeks, under a blond stubble of new whiskers, were glistening with tears. Little clumps of his thin light brown hair stuck out from his head like the dry stems of dead flowers. He whimpered, whined, rubbed his eyes, brushed his nose, and occasionally rocked back and forth in his chair, while the deadly serious game continued to play out.

At one point he moaned, "I wish I could give her back, but . . ." Saldana broke in, seemingly expressing earnest concern for the suspect's apparent agony: "Okay, no, I mean," he stuttered, "obviously you know she . . . she has gone on. I . . . I understand that."

Interrogation room confrontations between police and prisoners or suspects in the real-life arena of law enforcement are far different from the carefully dialogued scripts of movies or television series. In real life there are lots of starts and stops, "um-huhs," "buts," "ah, ahs," and "you knows." There are times when a complete sentence can be a rarity, and information most often leaks out a bit at a time in an elusively shifting fog of words.

Most of the time it takes several starts and stops to get at the truth, even when interrogators are successful. When Rathbun did talk about what happened to Linda, he was typically evasive and his story shattered, warped, and reshaped itself with all the hard-to-pin-down elusiveness of a greased pig. He dropped tiny fibs and glaring whoppers throughout the confrontation, but gradually step by painful step the experienced detectives dragged enough bits and pieces of the true story out of him to begin putting together a partial picture of what really occurred in the remote forest.

Saldana asked why Rathbun didn't tell him the truth about what happened to the model when they talked earlier in the day by telephone. The photographer replied that once he got started in a lie, he was stuck with it.

The detective leaned forward slightly and locked his eyes firmly on the suspect. "Look it, man," he said, "I would rather have you lie to me one time and then come in and we try to make things okay than to have her family have to see this on TV every day."

The confrontation between the detectives and the suspect continued on with fitful starts and stops. Saldana asked if it would help to return to the lake bed and the mountains and try to retrace his steps.

"It all looks the same out there. I just drove and drove and drove," Rathbun mumbled in reply.

Saldana and Bice urged him to do what he could to make things right and ease the pain of her grieving parents by leading authorities to the body so the young woman could be given a decent burial. They continued to work on whatever remorse the suspect might feel, concern for Linda's survivors, and to frame ghoulish descriptions of what was likely happening to her defenseless remains.

"And does she deserve to sit out there and have—" Saldana began.

"No, she doesn't," Rathbun quickly broke in. He knew exactly where the detective was headed with the question, but Saldana finished the sentence anyway ". . . you know, rip her apart. Because that's what they do in the desert. That's nature's way of cleaning up."

Bice interjected, bringing up the obvious way out: "And there's a possibility, you know, with . . . that, we could get out there before too much damage is done. But if we have to just wing it and wait for helicopters and search parties to go up there, who knows how long it will be?"

"Some hiker to stumble on, you know, some pieces of her in a couple, couple of months," Saldana added.

Rathbun indicated he was willing to lead searchers to the body—if he could find it again. He mentioned a cousin in Oregon who was a DA before moving to a job with the State Attorney General's Office. "There's a strong streak of right and wrong in my family," he pointed out.

The suspect also began to feel sorry for himself, moaning that the rest of his life was ruined. "Thirty seconds of . . . thirty seconds of fuck-up and the rest of your life is just gone," he moaned. He started to cry, and Saldana asked if he wanted a glass of water. Bice commiserated that it was an accident, and it had been Linda's "time."

"I'm so sorry for hurting her," Rathbun sobbed. Bice asked if there was a lot of blood. He responded that there wasn't much, just a little blood from a scrape on her ear. But she wasn't breathing. Her eyes were open and staring and he tried to pump her chest, he said, but he had never performed CPR before. Rathbun continued to whine that it was all over for him. He just bought a house and everything was going so good, he moaned.

"Look it, man, you're not a gang member. You're not a murderer. You're not a killer," Saldana coaxed.

"Yeah, I'm a killer. I killed a person," Rathbun miserably insisted.

"Yeah, but you didn't do it on purpose. Killers do it on purpose, man."

A bit later after Rathbun said he should have blown himself up like he thought of doing, Saldana assured him that would have been a mistake. What was done was done, the detectives indicated. Now he needed to do what was right.

Rathbun asked if he could talk to his friend Glenda Elam or to Shannon Meyer. Then he added Nichols's name and said he would like to tell all of them he brought them into the mess. "I should've just taken care of it myself. I don't know. Jim told me not to talk about it unless he was present. So I really should stop talking," he continued. "I said enough I guess."

While Rathbun was locked with the homicide detectives in the middle of one of the most important contests of his life, Nichols was spending most of his time alone in the nearby room. Whenever he had an opportunity to get the attention of someone, however, he demanded to be allowed to talk with the photographer. Detectives assured him he could meet with the suspect a bit later.

The interrogation continued, and the detectives briefly turned the conversation to the nonthreatening subject of celebrities Rathbun might have photographed. He said he shot pictures of lots of famous people including actors Mel Gibson, Charlie Sheen, and Sylvester Stallone, and actress Raquel Welch. Sheen and Emilio Estevez were in Hermosa Beach filming a movie titled, *Men At Work* when he photographed them. They were nice guys, he said. So was Mel Gibson.

"Sylvester Stallone is a prick," he added.

"Is he?"

"Yeah," Rathbun said. Then he began talking about Raquel Welch; her daughter, Tahnee; Paul Newman; and Jack Klugman.

The lanky, vomit-streaked man, slumped in the chair, made it clear a bit later that he wasn't dazzled by celebrity. "Most of these people are assholes. That's why I don't photograph celebrities," he volunteered.

"They're assholes?"

"Generally, yeah," Rathbun assured the two homicide cops. Celebrities were no big deal. Cars were what really excited him.

"Cars are what I do, what I do. I . . . they don't talk back and they aren't like . . . they are not like actors and actresses. They don't talk back. They don't have an attitude. They pay well, and that's the main thing . . . or they did, anyway."

The realization he was unlikely to be photographing any more cars for a long time, if ever, was still close to the surface of his consciousness. "Like you say, once you get a reputation as a killer you never . . . you don't work again," he said at one point. "So my life is over."

The conversation bounced around, focusing from one moment to the next on a variety of nonthreatening subjects ranging from the mundane, to the banal, to the trite. When Saldana admired his ring, Rathbun explained he had planned to use it at his wedding if he married some day, and that it was blessed by the Pope. "I'm not a Catholic, but what the hell, he was there."

The suspect was settling down, and for the moment at least seemed to have forgotten about talking to his lawyer. The gentle, sympathetic approach of the detectives was paying off, and it was time to bring the grueling ninety-minute ordeal of the interrogation to a close.

"He needs to go to the bathroom," Bice at last broke in. "But I just happen to have a brand-new map from the Antelope Valley. I mean, it's from the LA County area, and I could at least show you."

She glanced down at the crinkly paper while she spread the map out on the table in front of them and pointed her finger to an area of the desert at the forest's edge. "Here's the dry lake bed!"

Rathbun squinted his bloodshot eyes at the map, blinking and peering at the wriggly lines, and softly shaded colors. Then the prisoner and the police officers began narrowing down the search.

While Rathbun was busy at the Hollywood station, a team of detectives and evidence technicians drove to his house with a search warrant. The search, including close inspection of the suspect's own fully equipped photographic darkroom, was promisingly productive. Among the most intriguing, and ominous, discoveries was a cache of photographs of pretty models.

A personal computer complete with files was also among items seized during the search, and investigators were assigned to carefully check the records for clues and other information that might be helpful to the continuing investigation or during a criminal prosecution.

Armed with copies of the photographs of the models, during the next few days officers began checking with agencies and individuals in efforts to track down the women. Police wanted to know if they were alive, and if they were, homicide investigators were anxious to talk with them about the photographer and the circumstances that led them to model for him. Model portfolio cards found at the house were matched to some of the women in the photographs, and they were contacted and quickly eliminated as possible murder victims.

A warrant was also obtained for the white Lexus checked out from the manufacturer's fleet for the shoot, and it was impounded and hauled to the same sheriff's garage in Carson that Linda's sports coupe was taken to. Rathbun's personal car was still standing where he left it at the front of the house. A couple of days before the photographer's arrest, he spent hours giving the vehicle an especially thorough cleaning. Neighbor Bill Flanagan was impressed by the amount of time Rathbun devoted to the project. Flanagan later said Rathbun spent hours cleaning the vehicle inside and out.

When a team of detectives and evidence technicians at the sheriff's crime lab garage had an opportunity to comb through the shiny new prototype sports utility vehicle checked out of the Toyota fleet, they turned up still more evidence, including a small amount of blood and some strands of blond hair that appeared similar to Linda's. The blood and hair found inside the vehicle was carefully packaged, tagged, and scheduled for a closer look by crime laboratory analysts. Sophisticated DNA tests could be conducted with blood or tissue donated by her parents to determine with scientific exactness if the samples recovered from the Lexus came from the model—if investigators decided the process was necessary. A positive determination would establish a definite link between the missing woman and the photographer.

Disappointingly to detectives, neither the searches of the vehicle or of the house, turned up any photographs taken of Linda on the day she vanished. Authorities indicated later they didn't believe any pictures were even taken of her that day.

Alerted to some of the developments in the fast-breaking case, the media besieged Hermosa Beach police and the Sheriff's Department for information. Early Wednesday evening HBPD Lieutenant Mark Wright appeared at an outdoor press conference in front of the district station on Hollywood Boulevard and announced to a horde of reporters that the missing model might have been killed, and a suspect was in custody. Some of the reporters and cameramen stood or kneeled on large images of stars imprinted on the sidewalk along with the names of some of Hollywood's most revered actors and actresses. The press conference was held on movieland's renowned Walk of Fame, which annually attracts thousands of cinema fans and tourists. This time, however, the mass of humanity crowded onto the walk wasn't there to celebrate movie illusions, to relive favorite films, or to celebrate the careers of superstars. The reporters were there to gather information about the deadly reality of a missing persons investigation that was rapidly developing into a murder probe.

Flanked by fellow officers with the task force and standing in front of a tangle of microphones marked with identifying TV and radio station numbers and letters, Wright added that the suspect, Charles Rathbun, was arrested at his Hollywood home after attempting to commit suicide.

The press conference added new fuel to the rush by the media for still more information. While some reporters concentrated on law enforcement sources, others began knocking on the doors of Rathbun's neighbors. Reporters also telephoned or drove to the home of Linda's parents in Lakewood, while colleagues descended on the Denny's restaurant to interview staff and patrons.

Deputy Angie Prewett, a spokeswoman for the Sheriff's Department, also confirmed to the rush of reporters that Rathbun was in custody and was uninjured. "Apparently, he was planning to turn himself in to the authorities," she said. "There is a strong indication that a homicide has occurred."

In Hermosa Beach, Lieutenant Wright disclosed to reporters that Rathbun previously worked with the model, and she was seen getting into his car the day she disappeared.

Back at the Hollywood station it was early Wednesday evening when Nichols was at last permitted to talk with the woebegone, scruffy man who had been so abruptly thrust upon him as a client. Detectives advised the lawyer that Rathbun had given them a confession and wanted to help recover the body of the dead girl.

While a group of detectives outside huddled over a desk, intently peering at a big map of Los Angeles County, the lawyer was left alone in the interrogation room with his client and they talked for about fifteen minutes. Nichols was unaware that a tape recorder in the sound room was still running and saving every word uttered during their earnest conversation. When the detectives left the room so Nichols and Rathbun could have a private talk, they apparently forgot all about the tape recorder. It was a dreadful oversight with potentially serious consequences when the case moved into the courts and Rathbun's attorneys began examining police behavior and other aspects of the investigation in minute detail.

The miscue could be expected to be denounced by the defense as a violation of attorney-client privilege. In a worst-case scenario for the prosecution, everything Rathbun told the detectives as well as any other key evidence turned up as a result of his statements might be banned from the trial because it was considered tainted by the error. But that was a matter still to be decided, most likely at pretrial hearings. The officers involved later swore that they had not listened to the tape.

When Nichols emerged from the room, he advised the homicide cops that as a lawyer specializing in civil law, with no experience in criminal defense work, he couldn't continue representing Rathbun. Nichols had agreed with the photographer to represent him only until a criminal defense lawyer could be moved into the job.

Nichols asked the police officers to contact the Public Defender's Office and arrange for someone who was more qualified to take over as defense counsel. One of the detectives dialed a number and listened for a few moments before hanging up the receiver. Then the law officers asked Nichols to hang onto the job for awhile because they couldn't reach the public defender or anyone with that office. It was the Wednesday night before a holiday, and it appeared that no one was available. But police kept trying.

A few minutes later, Sheriff's Detective Ignacio "Nash" Reyes contacted an investigator with the Public Defender's Office and passed on the message. The investigator agreed to talk with a public defender and have him or her contact detectives at the Hollywood station.

At about 9 P.M., Deputy Public Defender Jane Marpet was contacted at her home and advised that an attorney was needed at the Hollywood station by a man suspected of killing missing model, Linda Sobek. Marpet talked by telephone with Reyes, and he told her Rathbun had already made a statement confessing to the killing and was asking for an attorney. Reyes related that the statement was made "outside Miranda," and added police wanted someone to talk with Rathbun in order to help pinpoint the location of the dead woman's body.

The detective was also quoted in court documents later filed by the deputy public defender as saying Rathbun was initially arrested by the HBPD for discharging a weapon, and that sheriff's investigators were called in to help conduct the probe.

When Marpet asked to speak with the defendant, Reyes put her on hold, then returned to the phone and said he would call her back. She gave him her phone number.

After a series of unsuccessful calls by Marpet and another deputy trying to locate a colleague on Miranda duty, or a colleague who lived close to the station, she decided to make her own inquiry. The public defender was considering driving to the Hollywood station but decided to wait for awhile for the call from Reyes. But when he called back he advised her the defendant wasn't available to talk with her at that time and added that Rathbun already had a civil lawyer with him. Marpet asked the name of the lawyer, then after being informed it was Nichols she said she wanted to talk with him. She said she could drive to the station in twenty minutes. According to the statement, Reyes put her on hold again, then returned a few minutes later and informed her that neither Nichols nor Rathbun were available to talk.

An hour or more had elapsed since Reyes' initial contact with the Public Defender's Office, and by that time Rathbun and Nichols had left with investigators to look around in the mountains for the body of the missing woman.

Investigators had explained to Nichols that they wanted to take Rathbun to a desert area to look for the girl. Nichols was unenthusiastic about the idea and wanted them to hold off until another lawyer who knew the ins and outs of criminal defense could be located to represent the suspect. But police were insistent. The lawyer reluctantly consented to the proposal but insisted that no one take Rathbun anywhere or ask him questions unless he (Nichols) was present. The lawyer strongly suspected that even if he didn't agree, police would take the suspect into the desert to look for the body anyway. By cooperating, he could at least accompany the suspect during the search and provide what help he could until another lawyer was lined up to take over the job of defense counsel.

Although Rathbun was shaken and suicidal earlier in the day, he seemed to have recovered better spirits and to be in a mood to cooperate with investigators looking for the body. It seemed he was an amazingly resilient man. But investigators also learned that he was a man who was once put on trial on charges of raping a woman acquaintance and acquitted, and whose later attitudes toward models he worked with got him into serious trouble with employers. Much of the adult life of the suspect was spotted with scrapes of one kind or another over rocky relationships with women.

THREE

A Rape Trial

Now Charles Edgar Rathbun stood accused of being one of the men with a camera that mothers warn their pretty daughters about.

Naive women with stars in their eyes traditionally have been tempted by smooth-talking con men who dangle the promise of celebrity and riches to lure gullible quarry into bed or into other compromising situations.

Phony movie producers, talent scouts, and assorted other self-proclaimed bigshots in the entertainment world are a dime a dozen at private parties, popular beaches, and college campuses—wherever young females with dreams of acting fame are likely to be found.

Other men-on-the-make use photography and the lure of professional modeling as their bait. Some are imaginative amateurs with twenty dollar cameras.

Rathbun was no amateur. He really was a professional photographer who utilized attractive models in his work, and he had an impressive portfolio to prove it.

Like Linda Sobek, the gorgeous model he would one day be accused of killing, Rathbun was a native of the Southern California sprawl around Los Angeles. He was born in the city on October 2, 1957, as one of a record-breaking 4.3 million babies arriving in the United States that year. Charles was the last of four children born to H. Robert Rathbun, a businessman; and to his wife,

Mary, a homemaker. All the siblings were spaced approximately two years apart. The oldest was Mary Ann, who was followed by a brother, Robert, then another sister, Louise.

The youngest member of the small brood was born almost exactly in the middle of the sign of Libra, the scales, and according to his horoscope he was supposedly destined to grow up as an individual who was orderly and persuasive.

President Dwight D. Eisenhower was in the first year of his second term, presiding over a period of industry, steady economic growth, patriotism, and firm national commitment to family values when Charles was born. The arts of the time reflected those values. In Hollywood a few miles from the hospital where the new baby made his debut, the movie industry was grinding out hits such as *Funny Face, Tammy and the Bachelor,* and *Paths of Glory,* as well as the film classics *The Bridge on the River Kwai* and *Twelve Angry Men. West Side Story* and *The Music Man* were the big hits on Broadway, and *The Ziegfeld Follies* was at last winding up an incredible fifty-year run.

All across the country young and old were listening to tunes like "Tammy," "Bye Bye Love," and cowboy balladeer Marty Robbins's classic about high-school romance and memories, "A White Sport Coat and a Pink Carnation." The literary world was humming with chatter about Jack Kerouac's *On the Road,* which is still considered to be the Bible of the Beat Generation; about Boris Pasternak's haunting story of love and the Soviet gulag, *Doktor Zhivago;* and Nevil Shute's frightening picture of nuclear holocaust, *On the Beach.*

The specter of a nuclear holocaust was still very real in the minds of many people. It was the middle of the Cold War and Americans were just beginning to build and stock personal family bomb shelters in anticipation of a nuclear face-off with the Soviet Union.

In the federal prison at Leavenworth, Kansas, Al Capone's old nemesis, George "Bugs" Moran, died quietly in bed of lung cancer, twenty-eight years after his near miraculous escape from the notorious Valentine's Day Massacre in a North Side Chicago carting garage.

In most ways, however, the middle 1950s were comparatively innocent times in America, and it was far too early for the squalling infant to be concerned about such matters as the quiet deaths of old-time hoodlums when he made the trip home from the hospital wrapped securely in blankets and his mother's arms.

Unlike Linda Sobek, Charles didn't spend all his formative years on the West Coast. He lived his teenage years as a Midwesterner. In 1969 his parents moved with their brood to a pleasant suburb of Columbus, Ohio. The slender, sandy blond haired boy was twelve years old, and he and his closest siblings spent much of their youth in Worthington. At that time the town was a quiet, largely residential community of about twelve thousand snuggled along the northern border of Columbus.

The town took its name from one of the earliest settlers in the old Ohio Territory, Thomas Worthington. The pioneer was one of a small group of New Englanders who helped carve a settlement out of the wilderness at the beginning of the nineteenth century. In 1803 Worthington became one of the new state's first two senators and later an Ohio governor. For a time it appeared that the busy business and manufacturing center that became his namesake community would be designated as the state capital, but it lost out to its hardier next-door neighbor immediately to the south. By the time the Rathbuns settled in the attractively affluent suburb—as is so commonly said about small-town America—it was a nice place to raise kids. It was quiet, safe, and composed of families that were firmly middle class, and almost solidly white.

Next door, Columbus was a thriving hub for high-tech industry and scientific information and a city of a half-million people with thousands more in rapidly burgeoning suburbs like Worthington, Upper Arlington, Whitehall, and Reynoldsburg. Located almost exactly in the middle of the Buckeye State, it was not only the state capital but was also home to the main campus of Ohio State University. Although in Ohio it was second in size to Cleveland by only a few thousand people, Columbus retained much of the flavor and appeal of a small town. And it was happily combined with cultural and other advantages of a big modern urban center.

OSU, which offered the cultural contributions of one of the nation's premier learning centers had a lot to do with that. Columbus is home to several other smaller colleges as well, including Bliss College, the Columbus Technical Institute, Columbus College of Art and Design, the Ohio Institute of Technology, and the Ohio Dominican College. But there were also other advantages besides educational opportunities that were reminders of Middle American small-town life such as the state fair held every August at the State Fairgrounds, the Columbus Motor Speedway, and car shows. A broad range of wholesome activities and attractions were available nearby when the Rathbun brood was growing up in the Midwest.

The local high school, named after the same favorite son as the suburb itself, Thomas Worthington, sponsored, among other activities, an ornithology club for fledgling bird watchers, and a bicycle club. Like many teenage males, one of the Charles's favorite pastimes was cruising in cars. The boy's interests and activities appeared to be about as normal as they could be. He didn't get into the drug scene, had no serious problems with alcohol, and didn't run off to become a flower child or involve himself in the nationally disruptive antiwar demonstrations that were flaring across the nation's colleges and many of the high school campuses at the time.

About the only unusual aspect of his behavior which friends could later recall when they looked back on what they knew of his youth was a curious attitude about his mortality. Rathbun claimed he knew from the time he was a boy that he would never live to the age of forty. The remarks weren't all that unsettling to his friends at the time, and it would be years before they were viewed as having any real significance. Later, viewed with hindsight, they would seem odd.

Although some of Charles's friends considered him to be fairly quiet and couldn't remember him doing any dating, he wasn't especially shy. He was at his best in groups of other male classmates, and that was when he appeared to be most relaxed and his personality became more outgoing, according to some of the recollections.

Charles was an average and undistinguished student. When he graduated from Thomas Worthington High School with the class of 1975, he had racked up a modest list of extracurricular accomplishments and activities. A photograph in his high school yearbook, the *Cardinal*, shows him as a typical appearing teenager. He is wearing glasses, has a tentative half-smile and a shock of wavy hair that is neatly combed back over his ears in a style that is fashionably long but cut shorter than that of most of his male classmates. A wisp of hair is curled over his right eye. There is nothing about the photograph that would make it stand out in any special way from that of any of the other boys.

He was also shown in his senior yearbook standing in the second row of a group of fifteen students who were staff members on the bi-weekly school paper, *The Chronicle*. He was a photographer for the newspaper. Years later a classmate who was news editor of the paper recalled him to a reporter as an aggressive journalist who was already an excellent photographer. One year Charles and his school newspaper pal took advantage of a break in classes to make a trip together to New York and New England.

By the time Charles completed high school, photography was one of the major interests of his life. If he had taken the trouble at the time to sit down and work out a formal ranking of the things that interested him most, photography, girls, and cars would probably have vied closely for first place. Photography had become such an obsession in fact, that when he registered as a student at OSU, he had already decided to become a professional shutterbug and make his living with a camera.

Rathbun signed up at OSU as a continuing education major, meaning that he wasn't a full-time four-year student. The program was set up to permit older students to register for a variety of classes and ease slowly into the college routine. Records available at the university for inspection are spotty and the recollections of faculty who taught or performed other functions there during those years are vague. Based on information available, it appears he never signed up for photo journalism courses or worked on the school paper, *The Lantern*.

Reports indicate that he managed to spend considerable time working in the darkroom and exchanging information dealing with the esoterics of the trade with other experienced photographers and enthusiastic neophytes like himself. In those days when just about anyone could stroll into *The Lantern* offices or other facilities of the journalism department and look like they belonged there, he was a regular in the photo lab. He also took other courses at OSU and while mixing jobs in the workaday world with a few classes, managed to log eleven semesters of part-time studies. That was far more semesters than the average for students working in a program that doesn't lead to a degree, and after all the effort he eventually managed to complete approximately two full years of higher education.

The OSU campus is about three miles northwest of the organized clutter of city, county, state, and federal government buildings that dominate the main central business area of Columbus and it was convenient to the part-time student. It was only a few minutes drive from his apartment in Columbus and from his workplace.

Rathbun had concentrated since his high school days on familiarizing himself with the intricacies of the photography trade. He soaked up all the special arcana that goes with taking pictures, developing the film, and printing photos. He learned what filters to use to bring out clouds in the sky so that they showed up sharp and clear or to present a moodier, more artistic atmosphere for his photos. He mastered composition and learned other secrets like using exactly the right shutter speed and film to stop action and capture a clear, sharp image of a speeding car; or allowing just enough light-streaks and fuzz in the photos to illustrate power and movement. He became proficient with darkroom techniques, blending his own chemicals until they were just the exact proper mix for the particular film he was developing; how to retain good image definition; how to make a good picture better by cropping; and various additional skills that are necessary and particular to his profession.

Although his father moved into management consulting, Charles's family wasn't wealthy and the young man was expected to work to help pay his own expenses. Freelance photography jobs provided one source of income. Employment at a hometown supermarket provided another.

He was working at a Kroger store in Worthington and his life appeared to be running a fairly steady course when he suddenly came to the serious attention of area law enforcement authorities for the first time. He was charged with raping a twenty-one-year-old married woman who worked with him at the supermarket.

According to the story recounted to police by the distraught woman, when she walked to the parking lot after completing her shift at the store on June 13, 1979, Rathbun was waiting by her car. He explained that his car had a flat tire and asked her to give him a ride to his apartment on her way home. It was almost midnight, a bad time to be stranded anywhere with a flat tire, and she agreed to play Good Samaritan. When they arrived at the apartment on Broadmeadows Boulevard in Columbus, Rathbun invited her inside for a few minutes to look at some photographs he said he wanted to show her.

The woman said she accompanied him into the apartment and looked over the photos. But when she turned toward the door to leave he suddenly grabbed her from behind. Alarmed and frightened, she demanded to know what he was doing.

''What do you think I'm going to do?'' he responded.

Moments later Rathbun began unbuttoning her blouse, ignoring her pleas for him to stop. She promised not to tell anyone what happened if he stopped and released her, but he ignored the pleas and forced her to the floor. Rathbun continued tearing at her clothes until she was stripped naked, she said. He told her he didn't want to hurt her but snarled that he would kill her if she made any noise. The supermarket clerk was in a terrifying situation. It was a few minutes after midnight, and she was naked and alone on the floor of the apartment with a sex-crazed man who outweighed her by about fifty pounds. No one else had any idea where she was or knew she was in trouble. There seemed to be every reason to fear he would back up his threat if she continued struggling. Rathbun raped her.

After the rape, he asked what she would like to do to him. The woman was hurt, humiliated, and angry, and her reply was scatalogically blunt and to the point. She said she wanted her husband to ''beat the shit'' out of him. When Rathbun told her she could put her clothes back on, she demanded he give her car keys back to her so she could leave. He planned to keep them for a while because he was going to drive her to some unspecified place, he reportedly told her.

After she dressed, they left the apartment together. He was walking her to the car when she began screaming at the top of her voice, then dropped to the ground. Rathbun scrambled after her, forcing his hand over her mouth and ordering her to calm down. Continuing the account, she said Rathbun asked her why she thought he raped her. Instead of waiting for an answer, he volunteered that he wanted to be punished for his disgusting behavior. He also told her that he was lonely and had told people he was sick, but no one believed him. It sounded as if in his mind, he saw himself as the principal victim of the affair, not the woman he had just raped.

The outraged young supermarket clerk wasn't in a mood to listen to apologies, excuses, or psychological musings by the man who just raped her. As soon as she got to her feet, accepted the car keys, and had an opportunity, she told her story to Columbus police. Patrolman John P. Bailey took down the details of the reported crime and drove the woman to University Hospital. She was examined and treated by Dr. William K. Rand, III, and a nurse, then released to her home. But the matter wasn't settled.

For the first time in his life, Rathbun was in serious trouble with the law. At about three o'clock Thursday afternoon, a few hours before he was scheduled to report for his shift at Krogers, he answered the telephone at his apartment. Walter Colflesh identified himself as an investigator with the Columbus Police Department and asked Rathbun if he was willing to voluntarily appear at the detective division there on Friday to talk about the woman's accusations. Rathbun agreed to a meeting and asked if he needed to bring a lawyer with him. The detective, who was assigned to the assault and sex crimes unit, replied that it was up to him. He could bring a lawyer if he wanted to.

It wasn't a difficult decision to make. There was no question that Rathbun needed a lawyer. But as a part-time college student who was working his way through school while supporting himself with occasional free-lance photo sales and a modest salary at a supermarket, he couldn't afford one. He left the apartment and drove downtown to the Franklin County Public Defender's Office and told the receptionist he had a problem with police and needed to talk with a lawyer.

His timing was bad. Like most public defenders, Franklin County's small team of lawyers who toil full-time at the job of representing indigent clients were up to their ears in work. Despite all of its attractions and advantages as a place to live, Columbus had its share of all the social ills and blemishes that affect most large metropolitan areas in America. Attorneys, paralegals, and other employees with the taxpayer funded office were faced daily with a flurry of cases that might typically include anything from shoplifting, car theft, and burglary to such serious major felony crimes as armed robbery, homicide—or forcible rape.

Totally evil, simply weak and irresponsible, or completely innocent, according to American law everyone charged with a crime has a right to legal counsel, whether or not they can afford to pay for it themselves. Public defenders who provide much of that counsel, labored under crushing caseloads. And when Rathbun walked into the Public Defender's Office there was simply no time in their busy schedules so late on that particular day to arrange for even one more appointment. If the young man wanted to talk to a public defender, he would have to arrange for a sit-down at some other time. It was a disappointing development and it appeared Rathbun would be keeping his appointment at the detective division without the benefit of a lawyer's advice or presence by his side. In the meantime, he had his Thursday night shift at Krogers to deal with.

Rathbun had barely walked into the store and tied and cinched a white apron around his skinny waist before one of his bosses showed up and ordered him to report to the front desk. A few minutes later he was informed that he was being placed on suspension until the matter of the accusations leveled by his fellow employee were cleared up. Then a team of officers from the Worthington and the Columbus police departments, who were waiting quietly a few feet away, stepped up. Curtly, in cold professional tones, the detectives advised him that he was being placed under arrest on a felony charge of rape.

The alleged rape occurred in Columbus, so it was their case. But the chain of circumstances leading up to the reputed crime began in Worthington, and the arrest was taking place there, so both police jurisdictions were involved.

It's doubtful if Rathbun was aware of or cared much about such delicate intricacies of local law enforcement at the time. Although the apprehension was carried out as quietly and efficiently as possible, the process was humiliating. The bespectacled young man left the store with his head down, walking uncertainly between two grim-faced policemen while other employees and a few puzzled customers peered curiously at him or whispered softly among themselves. It may have appeared that he was an accused shoplifter or someone who had tried to pass a bad check. But his problems were much more serious than either of those unpleasant possibilities.

In the parking lot of the store, Rathbun was helped into the backseat of a plain car. The driver turned out of the lot and headed south on High Street, then west to Interstate 73 and across the Worthington city line into the heart of the capital city. The ride to the old police headquarters, which at that time was just across a parking lot from the Columbus City Hall, was conducted silently, with no unnecessary chitchat. There was a need for some serious talk, but that was still a few minutes away.

It was shortly after 9 P.M. when Rathbun was led across the parking lot into the grimly intimidating old stone structure identified by a sign on the front as the DIVISION OF POLICE CENTRAL HEADQUARTERS. Inside, he was taken directly to an interrogation room in the Detective Bureau. Rathbun's stone-faced companions directed him to seat himself on a chair at a bare table.

Two homicide detectives, Robert Tormasi and David Cash, were waiting to question him. Tormasi wasn't much older than the suspect and had only been in the homicide unit about a month. Although the slender, nervous, bespectacled young man they were assigned to interrogate wasn't suspected of murder, homicide detectives often helped out their colleagues assigned to the sex crimes unit when it was justified by the workload.

According to later statements in legal documents, Rathbun asked if he could have a lawyer. The detectives told him there was no way they could get him a legal aid or public defender attorney until the next morning. Faced with the disappointing response, Rathbun signed a waiver of his rights to have an attorney present. Then he began to answer questions, relating his version of the story of what happened the previous evening in his apartment on Broadmeadows. Rathbun conceded that he and the young married woman engaged in sexual intercourse there but claimed the affair was consensual.

If the part-time college student expected to be driven back to the shopping center to pick up his car so he could return home to his apartment after his conversation with the detectives, he was disappointed. When the detectives at last pushed their chairs away from the table and directed him to stand, they led him to another area of the police building and turned him over to some of their colleagues. His name and a few other particulars were entered on the arrest log. Then he began moving through other stages of the formal booking process.

The fledgling photographer found himself on the other end of the camera, facing into the lens, then turning and posing for profiles. They were his first mug shots. Another technician led him through the ignominy of the fingerprinting process, expertly pressing the thumbs and fingers of his hands onto an ink pad, then rolling them one at a time onto heavy white cardboard sheets. His pockets were also emptied and his billfold, cash, and other small items he carried on him were inventoried, tagged, and stored in a secure locker. His property would be returned to him when he was released.

Finally, after responding negatively to brief questioning about any possible medical problems he might have which could require medication or special care, he was led to a spartanly furnished holding cell and locked inside. He spent the rest of the night by himself, alone with his thoughts and fears of the future.

Rathbun had his first talk with a lawyer the next morning, but it was July 29, more than two weeks before he was at last released from custody after posting bail through a local bonding company. By that time the slow, convoluted judicial process leading up to the proverbial day in court for himself and his accuser was already well underway inside the new Franklin County Courthouse at 369 South High Street. At the time, in the late 1970s, the gray stone structure with the black tinted windows was one of the most modern structures in the center of downtown Columbus. Reaching to a height of about fifteen stories it was also one of the tallest structures among the sprawling network of government buildings that dominated the downtown area.

After listening to testimony from the woman and other witnesses, a Franklin County grand jury returned an indictment against Rathbun for rape. According to the indictment, he violated the Ohio State Criminal Code by engaging "in sexual conduct, to wit: vaginal intercourse with (name of alleged victim), not his spouse, the said Charles E. Rathbun having purposely compelled (name of alleged victim) to submit by force, or threat of force."

By the time he appeared for arraignment, his attorney, Steven D. Rowe, of the Columbus law firm, Kept, Schaeffer and Rowe, was kicking up a fuss about the late-night statement his client made to investigators. Rowe contended the statement his client made to police was illegal because he was denied the right to have legal counsel present. It was the first time such a claim was made on Rathbun's behalf, but it wouldn't be the last.

While free on bail waiting for a conclusion to the case against him, Rathbun busied himself back at the university taking a few classes and hanging around in the photo laboratory where he continued to learn everything he could about his chosen profession. His work led to a meeting with a pretty redheaded, blue-eyed, OSU coed named Karen. She was also studying photography and one day about the middle of February when she walked into the lab to return a lens she had borrowed, a Valentine was waiting for her. It was from Rathbun.

Recalling the incident years later during an interview with a reporter for the *Columbus Dispatch,* she said he had written on the Valentine about staring into her eyes every time he saw her there. He also asked in the note if she would go out with him.

A week later he took her out to dinner. It was the beginning of a decade-and-a-half relationship that moved from friendship to romance, and back to platonic friendship. They barely began to date before Rathbun told her that he was involved in a problem with the courts over a rape charge. He cautioned, however, that she shouldn't believe everything she heard, and observed that women were known to "cry rape" lots of times. He was falsely accused, the photographer insisted.

Rathbun wasn't movie star handsome, but he was a good-looking young man. He was a slender six foot three inches tall, had a full shock of wavy light brown hair, and a pleasant sparkle in his eyes when he was in a good mood. Karen was impressed, and one thing led to another. Soon the auburn-haired beauty was posing nude for her photographer boyfriend. She also briefly became his lover. During one of the photography sessions she posed for him lying down with her eyes closed. According to her later recollections of the incident, he asked her to pose as if she were sleeping.

By the time she talked with police and the press years later about those particular shots, they had taken on ominous significance. Homicide detectives and backup personnel on the West Coast were already at work trying to locate other attractive subjects of the troubled shutterbug's busy lens whose photos showed them reclining with their eyes closed.

Acting on the advice of his attorney early in 1980, Rathbun waived his right to a trial by jury. Franklin County Common Pleas Court Judge Paul T. Martin presided at the bench trial. Rowe pressed his argument challenging the legality of Rathbun's early police statement and also argued that the sexual encounter that occurred between his client and the complainant was consensual. After listening to arguments from both sides, to witnesses, and considering other evidence, Judge Martin announced a verdict of not guilty.

Looking back on the case several years later and referring to his former client as "Charlie," Rowe told a newspaper reporter that Rathbun and the woman were fellow employees who went out for the evening, and whatever occurred was consensual. "There was no physical harm to the lady, and the judge believed Charlie was telling the truth," the lawyer said.

For the first time in months the possibility of being sentenced to prison was no longer hanging over Rathbun's head. But there was less to be thankful for on the romantic front. The love affair with the redheaded coed was rapidly sliding down the tubes. Soon after they began dating, his girlfriend met another young man and she broke off the sexual relationship. She wanted the two of them to remain friends, but there would be no more sex because she was in love with someone else, she explained to Rathbun.

That wasn't a development he found easy to accept, and although the former couple managed to continue their friendship the relationship was beset by problems. Rathbun didn't give up easily and he was determined to resume their former relationship as lovers, according to

Karen's later recollections. She found herself repeatedly fighting him off.

Despite being rejected so firmly and so often, Charles remained close to the young woman. Their friendship even survived her marriage to his rival and what she said was his continuing obsession with her after she became Mrs. Karen Masullo.

With his brief romance permanently ended, in 1981 Rathbun at last dropped out of college, packed up, and left Columbus. He traveled north to Detroit where he could work at the specialty he had chosen for himself, photographing cars and trucks.

FOUR

Michigan

The Motor City was the perfect place for an enthusiastic and bright young photographer with a special interest and talent for taking pictures of cars and trucks to build his professional career.

The broad-shouldered industrial city sprawled along the west side of the Detroit River was the center of the automotive world, the manufacturing Mecca for cars and trucks.

Pioneers of the industry such as Ford, Chrysler, Dodge, Nash, and Durant left their indelible stamp on the history and psyche of the city as well as on the business community. The names of the old auto barons, and those of their descendants are enshrined on the streets and highways, on public buildings, hospitals, and parks in the city and suburbs.

Every year the Motor City kicks off the summer season by hosting the Detroit Grand Prix, a race that draws some of the best cars and drivers in the world to Belle Island in the Detroit River at the mouth of Lake Saint Claire.

The metropolitan area is noted for such landmarks as the Edsel Ford Freeway, Greenfield Village and the Henry Ford Museum, the Pontiac Silverdome, Chrysler Building, and Cadillac Square, all reminders of the role the industry has played in the economic life and culture of the city. Auto plants and proving grounds, along with scores of subsidiary manufacturing operations are scattered throughout the area, and in Ontario, Canada, just across the river via the Ambassador Bridge or a short drive under the river through the Windsor Tunnel there are still more.

Rathbun couldn't have selected a more appropriate place at the beginning of the 1980s to start building his career and professional credits. He was surrounded by everything he cared for most. His world was photography, handsome new cars and trucks, and sleekly beautiful young women.

He thrived in Detroit—for a while.

Rathbun was meticulous, imaginative, and dedicated to his work. In 1985 he was hired by automobile advertising photographer Jim Haefner in the far north Detroit suburb of Troy as an assistant. He remained on staff about a year, refining his skills and expanding his contacts in the field of automotive photography.

He worked his way up to the job of senior assistant before leaving Haefner Photography in late 1986 and taking jobs for brief periods with other studios in the Detroit area. Every day spent shooting pictures of cars and trucks for advertising agencies and auto manufacturers added to his expertise and reputation as an outstanding young talent in his particular field of photography.

He also continued freelancing for his old employer both while he was still living in Michigan and later after permanently trekking west to California. He was a professionally respected member of the small fraternity of automotive photographers and maintained what may have seemed to someone less obsessed with his work to be a crushing pace.

In addition to shoots for former employers in and around Detroit, he freelanced assignments for *Motor Trend* in California and for other leading auto magazines published in Michigan and on the West Coast. General

Motors also became a good customer, although his assignments for them were made through agencies or other middlemen.

Attractive girls, sliding in and out of driver seats, holding open car doors, or lounging fetchingly in cutoffs or revealing bikinis often provided eye-catching props for his camera. With their long sparkling hair falling over their shoulders, the models smiled into the camera and posed prettily next to the open doors of shiny new Chevrolets and Cadillacs or draped languorously over the hoods of sleek Mercurys and Lincoln Town Cars. The contrast of the warm exposed flesh of the perfect female form and the cold polished metal and visual perception of power that was the linchpin of the motor industry showed off his talents at their best.

True to the reputation of the planet Venus and one of the major aspects of its namesake—the ancient Roman goddess of love and beauty which ruled his horoscope—Rathbun had become successful in a profession that permitted him to surround himself with lovely women. As an eligible bachelor, he capitalized on the opportunity to be in frequent close contact with the enticing females who modeled for him, as well as the proximity to other women working in or on the fringes of the twin automotive and beauty businesses.

He became involved in three or four longstanding romantic relationships during the years he worked in Michigan and went out on casual dates with various other women. But he never managed to form the kind of lasting partnership that would lead to marriage. The enigmatic photographer's personality and obscure motivations were as difficult to unravel and understand as an ancient Chinese puzzle. The man and his life posed a maze of contradictions.

Recollections of friends and business associates he was involved with vary, but although he was considered to be friendly and social by some, there were times when his personality would turn perplexingly sour. He didn't exhibit much patience when things went wrong. Even minor failings or mistakes on the part of a model or a problem with his equipment could lead to fierce temper tantrums, according to associates from those days.

After the shocking story of the California model's violent death was flashed across the country by the media, Denise Strong, a woman who knew Rathbun when he worked in Troy, recalled him to a reporter as "a wonderful guy." Her husband, Ron, had worked at the studio with Rathbun. Mrs. Strong also said she didn't know Rathbun to have any girlfriends, but indicated his busy work schedule could have had something to do with that. "They would work from dawn to sunset," she told the *Detroit Free Press*.

William Powell and his wife, Pamela, who were former associates in the auto photography business, had a longtime friendship with Rathbun and talked of pleasant memories. William stated during a television interview on WJBK in Lansing that Rathbun ". . . was never violent or anything like that in any way. That's why we liked him . . . still like him." Mrs. Powell said Rathbun was comfortable with men and with women. He was a social person who dated as often as could be expected, considering his work and his frequent traveling, she recalled.

But Haefner, Rathbun's former boss, said the photographer "didn't have great relationships with women. He didn't seem to have any girlfriends."

Some women who worked with Rathbun or had business dealings with him described their reactions to the photographer with words and phrases such as "uncomfortable" and "bad vibes." One woman said although he never made passes at her or said anything improper, she just wasn't at ease around him.

To at least some of his associates, he was remembered as a brooding loner who sometimes stayed with his divorced mother in the small suburb of Beverly Hills a few minutes drive south from Pontiac and collected guns. The living arrangement ended when his mother remarried and moved out of state, but Rathbun continued his preoccupation with guns and at one time put together a miniarsenal of ten or more. He was likely to spend his free time tinkering with guns, immersed in some intriguing new facet of the burgeoning complexities of his vocation, or simply to be enjoying his cat, Butt-Head, while watching adventure and old rock-n'-roll movies. He didn't have a reputation for frittering away long nights on the town drinking and dancing.

Rathbun was also reluctant to give up his former girlfriend in Columbus, and at times seemed to be more interested in trying to rekindle the old, cold romance from his college days than in seeking a loving relationship with someone new. Even though Karen had married another man, he continued to talk with her every few months by telephone. Occasionally he telephoned more often. And every couple of months or so, she would also receive a sexually suggestive card from him.

On his frequent trips back to Columbus to see members of his family or to attend the Columbus International Auto Show and similar events at the Veterans Memorial, he usually managed to spend some time with her. Although she cared enough about the friendship to keep up contact with him, his continued sexual aggressiveness was a problem that couldn't be ignored. The five foot two inch tall, 110-pound woman was careful not to get herself in situations where she was alone with him.

When Karen inquired about the models he worked with and the state of his love life, as often as not, he would mutter something about their airheadedness and inability to see past the outer shell to the real man inside. He made nasty cracks about the beauties, who were usually blondes, referring to them as all dark roots and silicone. Judging from his remarks he considered most of the models he worked with to be insubstantial phonies with more hair spray than brains.

Rathbun was continuing to develop an unpleasant reputation among some of the models in Michigan. Modeling agencies are protective of their clients, and word of rogue photographers who are sexually aggressive, bully models, or whose behavior is otherwise troubling and suspicious, gets around in a hurry.

Rathbun's work problems with models had the potential to seriously hinder his career. The quality of his photography was so good, though, that some of his contacts in the trade, including *AutoWeek,* continued using him for freelance jobs. He also did occasional jobs for some of the big car manufacturers including General Motors and Oldsmobile. But not many of the photo shoots involved models. Eventually, the photographer packed his personal cameras and other photo equipment in his car along with his clothes and a few other items, then drove eighty-five miles northwest along Interstate 96 to Lansing. Rathbun apparently moved briefly into a mobile home park in East Lansing, a near suburb that abuts the capital city on the southeast border. In some documents he filled out in June 1993 he listed his address as 2700 Eaton Rapids Road, in suburban Delhi township.

Like Columbus, Lansing was also a state capital city of about a half-million people, and home to a major Midwestern center of learning, Michigan State University. If Rathbun cared to follow the football fortunes of his alma mater during the season when the "Buckeyes" were on the road playing the local favorites, it was only a short drive from the trailer park to the stadium in East Lansing. During the basketball season, there were similar opportunities to watch the OSU hoop squad match their skills with the "Spartans" of MSU. More importantly, coeds at the university could presumably provide a good source of amateur models.

Lansing shared yet another similarity with Columbus and with Detroit. It was a river city. When Lansing was first planned in the 1830s it was located at the juncture of the Red Cedar and Grand rivers. But Rathbun was less interested in the topography and beauty of the city than he was the opportunities it offered, and one of those was its easy accessibility to his old stomping grounds in Detroit. When photo opportunities opened up for him in the Motor City he could make the drive along the freeway in a little more than an hour—with plenty of time to do the shoot and return home the same day.

Air terminals were also handy. The Capital City Airport in Lansing, and the Detroit Metropolitan Wayne County Airport in a suburb of the Motor City were only a short drive away from the mobile home court in Delhi township. That was important, because as he began building up his freelance business he traveled frequently, not only in the Michigan area, but also on longer jaunts to the West Coast, most often to Los Angeles.

When he was in Los Angeles on location he stayed in hotels and much of his early indoctrination into the area was soaked up through chats with bartenders and barmaids. Like many newcomers and tourists, he was given a classic welcome to the city by a thief who cleaned out his car on his very first day in town. That was a minor problem that could have happened anywhere. More importantly, Los Angeles offered a fertile range of opportunities for a good photographer with Rathbun's skills and particular specialities. An attractive scatter of automotive magazines was published in the city and the suburbs located throughout the valleys and coastal area.

There were also California girls—homegrown lovelies, and thousands of other acting and modeling hopefuls from around the world who were attracted to the City of Angels by its proximity to the international film capital, along with other alluring opportunities linked to the thriving advertising and publishing industries.

His work increasingly took him to the West Coast. Soon he was spending considerably more of his time in California than he was in Michigan. He had earned a reputation among executives with area auto magazines as an excellent photographer whose sharp, clean pictures always showed new and customized vehicles at their shiny best.

His reputation among the models he worked with or discussed using for shoots was less sparkling. Beautiful females who often pose in scanty bikinis, lingerie, or less for photographers, tend to develop impressions about the people they work with that in some ways are almost psychic. If they want to stay out of trouble they have to play their hunches, as well as use their native intelligence and common sense.

Whether or not it was sheer intelligence, an ability to read body language, or a mysterious protective feminine intuition, there was something about the tall, bespectacled automotive and calendar photographer that struck a number of them as being disconcertingly strange or off center. They weren't comfortable with him. Years after meeting him some of the models, along with other women who had crossed paths with Rathbun even though they were not in the modeling business, they told police investigating the Sobek affair that he made passes at them, looking for sex. They talked about his persistence, even after they turned him down. He wasn't a man who gave up easily.

According to his old friend Karen in Ohio, he had a history of attraction to women who weren't interested in him. He had lots of crushes on lots of women, she told the *Columbus Dispatch*. "That was a constant pattern for him."

But like his reputation in the Midwest, his reputation in California in regard to his personal life and behavior, depended on who you talked to. Nancy Hoogenhuis, a publicist, told the *Los Angeles Times*, Rathbun tried to date her when they talked during an auto event she had organized. Although he was polite and said he had two tickets to *Phantom of the Opera*, she begged off. The publicist was tired after working all day. Rathbun didn't behave any different than most other men might in accepting the turndown, she recalled. He asked another woman working at the same event, and she went out with him.

Despite the difficult manner Rathbun reputedly sometimes exhibited to models and other people he rubbed shoulders with as part of his professional life, jobs in California and freelance shoots back in the Midwest helped him earn a good living for himself. He spent increasingly more time in California, but he wasn't yet ready to totally sever his personal and professional ties in the Midwest.

He hung onto a Michigan driver's license for years, keeping it until his thirty-sixth birthday in 1993 when he at last permitted it to expire. For at least a couple of years he had driver licenses both in Michigan and in California. He also continued his frequent visits to the Midwest and kept his mail address in Delhi township. *AutoWeek,* one of the top automotive magazines in the country was headquartered in Detroit, and the slick publication continued to be one of his best freelance markets.

Rathbun was a regular at the major auto shows, not only in Columbus, but all around the country. He traveled a few miles outside Los Angeles for events like the Inland Empire International Auto Show in San Bernadino, and he made longer trips to shows in and around Detroit and anywhere else that offered opportunities for him to photograph new model cars and cement his relationships with editors, publicists, and various other people in the trade.

As the decade of the 1980s was nearing a close, he accepted a full-time job as a staff photographer with the Petersen Publishing Company. The publisher, based on Los Angeles's trendy Wilshire Boulevard, produced a large package of about seventy-five magazines devoted to automotive enthusiasts including *Motor Trend, 4-Wheel Off the Road,* and others.

Several of the magazines used cover photos or inside pictures of sexy models in bikinis or shorts, posing fetchingly next to customized cars and trucks or seated on sleek motorcycles. The magazines offered a perfect vehicle for Rathbun to show off his special skills in automotive photography. Officially, he went on staff and the company payroll on February 8, 1989.

California offered a bright new opportunity to start over while continuing to work at the kind of job he liked best.

FIVE

California

Rathbun slid quickly and easily into the routine of his new duties.

He was experienced and talented and the quality of his work, which began regularly appearing in the package of slick automotive magazines, rapidly made him a favorite with the publishing group.

If the ability to do a good job and produce fine work as a staff photographer for *Motor Trend* was all that was involved, Rathbun may have climbed even higher in the organization. But his personality made him difficult to work with. He tended to be overbearing and pompous, and had a self-important attitude about his work that sometimes made it appear as if he believed he was the only person who knew how to do a job and could do it right. He wasn't a big favorite with models.

Even his friend in Columbus, Karen, wasn't immune from the brusque surliness and pomposity. One time when they were talking by telephone and she asked him to show a friend around the Los Angeles area, he responded with a nasty tongue-lashing. He complained that he was fed up with people taking advantage of him and wouldn't permit her to exploit their friendship. They didn't speak again with each other for two years after the outburst, but eventually resumed contact. Nevertheless, Mrs. Masullo was troubled by what she perceived to be an ominous change in her longtime friend's personality.

Early in the new decade of the 1990s Karen read about a string of mysterious vanishings of young women on the West Coast and briefly considered contacting police to tell them about Rathbun. Ultimately, she decided against it because she told herself Rathbun couldn't be a killer. There was no question Rathbun was a bit strange, but so were a lot of other people.

Despite Rathbun's responsibilities on the West Coast, he continued to shuttle back and forth to Michigan and maintained a busy shooting schedule for automotive customers there. The Oldsmobile Division of the General Motors Corporation in Lansing was one of his better Midwestern customers and provided him with assignments off and on for a couple of years while he was maintaining his base in California.

One of the better qualities his associates and small circle of friends noticed about him was his high energy level. Regardless of his frequent crankiness and occasional quarrels with models and others, no one could fault him for dragging his heels when it came to work. Despite his frequent trips back and forth between the West Coast and the Midwest, he kept up with or surged ahead of his colleagues, and consistently produced top-notch work. Hobbled by a bulging suitcase and an armload of photographic gear, he was a familiar sight struggling through crowded terminals at the Los Angeles International Airport, the Detroit Metropolitan Wayne County Airport, and the Port Columbus International Airport.

Rathbun's free-and-easy bachelor life provided him with the freedom to travel where and when he wished to, without the intrusion of family responsibilities. There was just himself and Butt-Head to worry about, and when the photographer was away from home for a while there was always someone handy who was willing to feed the cat and freshen his litter box.

Occasionally Rathbun's work took him out of the country, and he spent several days one summer in Sicily with Steve Spence, the managing editor of *Car and Driver* magazine. Rathbun guided a new Mustang over the Targa Florio racecourse there, testing the tires. Spence didn't notice a thing about his companion to indicate he was anything but a normal male.

Rathbun was comfortable with other men in the business and enjoyed boys nights out at local watering holes where he could exchange talk and observations about photography, cars, guns, and women. They were his passions, especially anything to do with the automotive world. He could sit for hours nursing a couple of beers and talking about such vehicular exotics as V6 engines, dual suspension systems, overhead camshafts, foot-pounds of torque compared to rates of rpm, and the bold and exciting engineering of new model cars and trucks.

Most of his friends were people he associated with in the automotive photography business, and he didn't go out of his way to socialize with neighbors and others who didn't share his professional interests. When he rented a neat three-bedroom house on Canyon Drive in Hollywood, he didn't seek out contact. He had a roommate, and his own friends.

His landlady, Christian Kilpatrick, was young and single, and they dated for awhile but broke up after a few months. Years later she reflected on the relationship, during an appearance on the television talk show *Leeza* and in an interview carried by the supermarket tabloid *Globe*. Ms. Kilpatrick said she broke up with Rathbun because he was "weird" and "creepy." She recalled stumbling onto a secret A-frame room in the attic she hadn't even known existed, where he kept his guns and pictures of naked models. Similar stories were recounted by other women to different reporters and to law enforcement authorities as public interest in the complex, enigmatic photographer mushroomed in the aftermath of the missing model mystery.

Stunning "Penthouse Pet" Samantha Phillips told the *National Enquirer,* she rejected an offer from Rathbun to pose nude in a remote area only a couple of weeks before Linda vanished. The statuesque model said she turned him down after he said he wanted to shoot some artistic studies of the nude form in a natural setting, then explained he would only photograph her from the neck down. He told her he only wanted to take pictures of what he referred to as "body parts," she said.

Ms. Phillips said the bizarre suggestion gave her "the chills," and she firmly refused.

Another model, twenty-four-year-old Tia Smith was quoted in the same story saying she was frightened away by the photographer two years earlier. Rathbun showed her a portfolio of "body parts" pictures, then asked her to wear a dog collar for some shots. She got away from him as fast as she could, Tia said.

Rathbun didn't appear to be especially unfriendly, he simply didn't go out of his way to strike up new friendships with people just because they happened to live a few doors away. He didn't show up at the frequent neighborhood parties, but there were times when he chatted with next-door neighbor Bill Flanagan and other nearby residents about matters of shared interest.

The photographer was a handyman, who tinkered around the house, building tables, putting up shelves, and keeping up with the lighter maintenance work that's part and parcel of being an owner or renter of a home. The house was his special refuge, and after renting for several years, he put a deal together and bought it. He was still a bachelor but he had moved firmly into middle age, and for the first time was putting down the kind of serious roots that go along with ownership of a home. It needed some work, and he began dealing with the problems one project at a time.

He also took care of many of his own car repairs, personally dealing with the smaller mechanical problems that developed, and kept his vehicles washed and polished to bright shines. The cars he drove always carried Michigan license plates or dealers tags. A time or two neighbors noticed him outside the house in the early postmidnight hours planting trees in the yard.

The quiet residential street was in a friendly neighborhood. Even though a short jaunt to the end of Canyon Drive leads to the famous "Hollywood" sign in the Hollywood Hills that evokes the image of so much Tinseltown glamour, movie stars and big-time producers don't make their homes there. They live in tonier, more expensive neighborhoods and communities such as Bel Air, Beverly Hills, and Brentwood.

If Rathbun's neighbors were to be labeled according to their socio-economic status, they could probably best be characterized as firmly upper-middle-class. Most were professional people. They visited back and forth, and their children played in each other's backyards. But most of the nearby residents apparently didn't even knew what kind of work Rathbun did for a living, although he was often seen with photo equipment. Sometimes other men loaded down with photography gear trooped into the house with the occupant. Neighbors saw Rathbun loading or unloading rifles or gun cases in and out of his car about as often as they saw him with cameras, tripods, and other photo equipment. For all they knew, the cameras could have been nothing more than the gear of a dedicated amateur photographer who entertained himself snapping pictures of birds, boats, or landscapes.

Occasionally, attractive women were noticed by observant neighbors to be visiting at the house. Early in November 1995, an especially good-looking young woman with long, golden blond hair drove up in a late-model white car, climbed out, and walked confidently inside.

When other residents of the area ran across the tall, bespectacled recluse in a local store, he barely acknowledged them and seldom had more than two or three words to say. He didn't even open the windows of his house to catch the occasional breeze slipping down from the Hollywood Hills. In the early fall of 1995, he installed iron security bars on the outside of his windows. By that time Butt-Head, the feline companion he dragged across the country with him, had been dead for several months.

Rathbun was lonesome and continued to seek close female companionship. But he was still a nasty loser in the game of love. No one likes rejection, and on the frequent occasions when he was turned down by a woman he approached for a date the moody photographer could turn exceedingly ugly. Some of his female coworkers complained to their bosses about sexual harassment.

A colleague who was art director for Petersen Publishing recalled after Rathbun's arrest in the Sobek slaying that he hounded women who worked at the office for dates and refused to accept their brush-offs when they didn't choose to go out with him. He pushed and persisted, continuing to pester them to change their minds. Some of them did, or their initial response was positive, and by late 1995 he was dating an attractive woman who worked at Petersen.

But he was frightening to at least some of his female associates at the magazine. One of the women, a secretary, was later quoted as saying his eyes had the appearance of looking right through other people. When he lost his high-voltage temper, which could occur anytime he didn't get his way or other problems developed, according to some of his coworkers he metamorphosed into another completely different and sinister personality that was as immediately threatening as jangling concertina wire.

His male coworkers weren't shielded from his cranky moodiness either, and were sometimes witness to ugly flares of temper. Bob D'Olivio, the company's director of photography, said his hotheaded associate was known for erupting in tantrums. One day he flew into a fit of anger and hurled an office chair across the studio. When things went wrong for him Rathbun wouldn't admit the problem might be his own fault. Instead, he was more likely to blame the troubles on somebody else or on the equipment, D'Olivio recalled. Despite Rathbun's obvious abilities and topnotch performance as a photographer, his skills were overshadowed by his atrocious behavior. He didn't respond well to supervision and had a habit of doing things his own way, regardless of how his bosses wanted it done.

Except for one relatively minor incident, however, his troubles didn't involve the law and there was no repeat of anything even approaching the seriousness of the rape charges brought against him in Columbus. Nevertheless, he had a couple of run-ins with street people that might have developed into serious violence, but stopped just short of actual combat. On each occasion, according to his account, he was working when someone threatened him with a knife or similar weapon.

One time he was on a job in Pomona with a friend when he got in line at a McDonald's next to a boy about ten years old who was talking to some other youngsters. Moments later the boy, whom he described as "a little gang-banger" walked up to him and snarled in his child's voice, "Old man, don't fuck with me or I'll shank you." While his companions watched admiringly, the child pulled his shirt back to show a knife, then he pulled it out to prove he meant business.

Sometime after that a bum in LaBrea threatened Rathbun with a screwdriver before breaking off the brief confrontation.

One day he was at the corner of Vine and Melrose preparing for a photo shoot when a psychotic bag lady who was seeing or hearing things that disturbed her, waved a knife at him. And another time he walked out of a studio on Sunset Boulevard in Hollywood just as an industrious thief was absorbed in the task of breaking into a car parked at the curb. Both of the men were startled, but when Rathbun tried to retreat back into the studio he realized the door had locked behind him. The photographer backed against the wall as the car burglar menaced him with a screwdriver, but after a few tense moments the thief slunk away.

No one was hurt in any of the confrontations, and they were merely part of life as it's lived by someone in Los Angeles every day. Fortunately for Rathbun, he was young, healthy, and strapping tall. Even though he was no brawler, and with his round, wire-rim glasses and placid face he looked comfortably unthreatening, there was obviously easier prey on the streets.

The only time he came to police attention in California, he got in trouble for pulling a truck across a highway and impeding traffic without a permit. He was using the truck on a photo shoot, and true to the seriousness and total absorption he always showed when he was working at his job, in his anxiety to obtain exactly the photographs he wanted, he stepped across the line of what was permissible and what wasn't.

Ultimately, on April 27, 1992, he appeared in court and admitted impeding travel, while entering a plea of no-contest to the misdemeanor charge of violating a Los Angeles County civil ordinance. The judge ordered a suspended 180-day jail sentence, with one-year summary probation, and assessed a fine of $1,370.

Less than two months later, Rathbun was finally fired from his job at Petersen Publishing. Typical of the enigmatic, profoundly complex man, when his dismissal was discussed with reporters a few years later two quite different reasons were given. It was first said that his firing was tied to claims of sexual harassment. A short time later Petersen executives released a statement asserting he was let go because of staff reductions. Whatever the reason, or reasons, for his leaving, he had managed to hang onto the same full-time job for nearly three and a half years. It was a record for him.

Once more the talented but painfully irascible photographer found himself without a regular paycheck, and facing the pitfalls of making a living as a freelancer. It was a seat-of-the-pants task that depended on guts, persistence, contacts, and personal salesmanship as much as talent and the technical skills of his profession.

The pay was good when he had work. The going rate for a day of shooting was about $350, although that could vary depending on the job and the hours spent. There were also opportunities to double up on the pay by shooting a job for a client and taking additional pictures to be freelanced to other markets. The downside of the picture was the erratic nature of assignments. One week he might have only a single day of work, and the next he might book jobs on four or five days. The inconsistency of available shoots was a problem he shared with the models he sometimes worked with. For a while he worked with an agent in nearby Montebello and impressed her with his professionalism and industriousness.

Wisely, he kept his skills up-to-date and on top of the rapidly improving leading edge technology in photography. He easily mastered the intricacies of operating in computerized darkrooms, learning such newly emerging tricks-of-the-trade as how to use electronics to make cars and trucks that were stationary seem to be spinning wheels and kicking up gravel or dust. Rathbun's dedication and enthusiasm for his work came through in his photographs. He was very good, one of a select handful of truly excellent automotive photographers who knew how to capture the pulse-pounding beauty of machines mounted on rubber and constructed of metal and glass. Through his own knowledge, imagination, and his camera lens he magically translated the thrill and excitement of car buffs into still pictures with three-dimensional quality that seemed to jump right off the page.

But his old troubles followed him as a freelancer and according to later reports, at least one magazine, *Hot Rod*, discontinued using his work after complaints from models about his behavior. But there are scores of magazines devoted to the various elements of the automotive world, and many of them are based in the Los Angeles area. Furthermore, Rathbun knew his market. He had the knowledge, the skills, and the contacts necessary to be a successful freelancer. As 1995 began to wind down he was still busy and making a good living at his trade.

Back in the Midwest the late summer air was beginning to reveal faintly cool hints of the approaching autumn, but the first frost was still days away and the leaves weren't yet changing color when Karen Masullo talked by telephone with her photographer friend about some pictures she posed for years earlier. Rathbun said he wanted to use some photos in a show of her reclining on a couch. They were the most beautiful pictures he ever shot of her, he said.

The photographer didn't call her again, but she had reason a few weeks later to remember her last conversation with the strange man she had considered for so long to be one of her best friends. By that time early autumn frosts had turned the leaves on trees in central Ohio to brilliant reds, yellows, oranges, and ochre, before they crinkled up and dropped off leaving branches that were gray and bare. Pedestrians and motorists on the streets of Columbus were bundling up in heavy jackets and coats, and brisk breezes were whipping across the campus at OSU and nipping at noses and ears when Charles Rathbun made national news.

He was in jail in California, suspected of murdering a beautiful blond model.

SIX

Linda

Linda Elaine Sobek was the quintessential California girl.

She was a confident young woman of the nineties, but in some ways she was also a charming throwback to the placid days of the 1950s when beach bunny movies and pop music songs were composed around lithe young beauties just like her.

Linda had it all, a storybook life set in the picturesque South Bay, barely a heartbeat from the exciting lure of Los Angeles and Hollywood; one a leading media and advertising center, and the other the movie capital of the world.

She was a stunningly beautiful woman with baby blue eyes, long golden hair, the kind of dazzling smile seen most often in toothpaste ads, the svelt figure of a young goddess, and a bubbly, loving personality. The only daughter of Robert and Elaine Sobek, an engineer and a homemaker, she was the baby of a classic nuclear family that included an only sibling, her older brother, Steve.

She grew up healthy, happy, and pixie cute in a working-class neighborhood in Lakewood, one of the disorganized sprawl of bedroom communities ringing Los Angeles, about a fifteen-minute drive from the Pacific Ocean. Linda was born in a hospital in the neighboring community of Norwalk on July 9, 1968, under the astrological sign of Cancer. People born under that sign are generally believed to be sensitive, impressionable, and sympathetic. They were all qualities that would show up in Linda's personality.

The little girl loved animals, and her affection for cats, dogs, and other pets was a lifetime trait. As a young adult she had a houseful of pets, at one time including a pride of cats—Thrasher, Princess, and Tigger, a raven, and a Doberman named Boo. She especially admired the grace and sensuous power of cats and wrote that her favorite animals were tigers.

She was a typical girl, with a special love for the outdoors. Neighbors were used to seeing the child, her mop of natural blond hair bleached nearly white by the sun, outside her house roller-skating along the sidewalk, riding her bicycle, playing hopscotch, or fussing with her dolls.

Linda also liked playing big sister, and sometimes visited the house of an older married cousin to take care of his younger children, brushing the little girl's hair and playing with the boy. As she reached junior high school and high school age she was a favorite neighborhood baby-sitter.

During her teenage years she was one of the most popular girls at Artesia High in nearby Cerritos. Linda had the kind of fresh good looks and effervescent personality that made high school boys choke up, forget their own names, and stumble into open locker doors. But she was also well liked by her female classmates and formed close friendships with some of them that lasted throughout the rest of her life.

Her curly hair was as yellow as fresh dandelion blossoms and when she smiled, which was most of the time, diamonds of light danced in her eyes. Experimenting along with her girlfriends, she learned to augment her awesome natural beauty with just the right touch of lipstick, flick of mascara, or eye shadow. But as a teenager, the exotics of makeup was reserved for special occasions. She didn't need it. From the time she first began blossoming into the full beauty of womanhood, the natural look best fit the radiant schoolgirl. She looked as crisply clean and refreshingly innocent as a Mouseketeer.

Linda performed with her high school drill team at parades and football games and took an active role in other extracurricular activities. During her final two years in high school, she was a varsity cheerleader. She had to work hard to master the graceful, athletic moves that look so easy when they're done properly. Recalling Linda's early efforts at learning the spins, twirls, jumps, and other gyrations, Elaine Sobek told *People* magazine her daughter was a bit of a klutz. Sometimes it was hard to keep from laughing when Linda bounced and pirouetted around the room, she confided.

But she kept at it, and soon she was performing the precision demanding cheerleading acrobatics with picture-perfect timing and skill. Like her fellow members on the school pep squad, she was part athlete, part showgirl. From the time she was a small child she was active and enthusiastic about exercise and set her sights early on becoming a cheerleader. When neighbor boys who were about her age and lived just across the street organized scrub games of tag football, Linda stationed herself on the sidelines and provided the cheerleading.

While growing up she was more likely to spend time working out, practicing cheers with her pom-poms and megaphones, or playing beach volleyball with mixed teams of other girls and boys, than parked in front of a droning television set placidly blinking her eyes and munching calories. During free weekends and the lazy summer days that broke up the school year, Linda often headed for the Strand, a broad cement walkway flanked by the soft yellow sandy beach and trendy shops that was a favorite gathering place for active teenagers and young adults. The Strand stretches from Redondo Beach through Hermosa Beach at the south edge of Santa Monica Bay. There she could bicycle, in-line skate, jog, or join her peers in other outdoor activities.

One of the favorite activities was joining other teenagers sprawling on beach blankets spread out on the yellow sand, and luxuriating in a carefree world of suntan lotion, bikinis, portable radios, hot dogs, and potato chips. Linda grew up surrounded by sunshine, surfers, and soft, warm sand squishing between her bare toes. By the time she was high school age, she had learned to climb onto water skis and giddily swoop and bounce in the wake of a speedboat, or to guide her own jet ski over the tranquil sky blue waters of Santa Monica Bay.

She was already entering and winning beauty contests while she was in high school, and on the rare occasions when she didn't win she placed close to the top. In 1985 when she was a seventeen-year-old high school senior, she competed in the Miss Lakewood contest and lost by a hair. She was the runner-up.

She also began modeling during her junior year of high school. She was sixteen when she worked her first modeling job, and incredibly, she was already playing catch-up with younger girls. In the big-time modeling world of today, girls often begin working before they're out of junior high school. Lonneke, one of the most popular models with the busy New York agency, Paulines, was already climbing to the top when she was only fourteen. Christy Turlington, a leading international runway model, was thirteen when she was "discovered" by a photographer.

However, even at sixteen, Linda was still young enough to launch a successful modeling career. But she had a more serious problem than her age to surmount. She was about four inches shorter than the average height of the tall, leggy models who dominate the business. Linda called on her vivacious personality to deal with the problem, and quickly became a favorite with clients. Her charisma and bubbly charm paid off and were translated into the pictures she posed for.

She was a born achiever, in and out of the classroom. If she set her mind on accomplishing something, she carried it out. Throughout her high school years she maintained a respectable grade average, and her scholastic record was high in the top half of her class when she graduated in 1986.

Despite her beauty and natural enthusiasm, Linda experienced many of the normal teenage problems. Her most serious crisis occurred when she was seventeen and sliced a tiny, hesitant cut in her left wrist during a fit of despondency after breaking up with a boyfriend. It didn't seem to be a serious attempt at self-destruction, but she incurred some light tissue damage that stayed with her the rest of her life. The foolish schoolgirl act seemed grossly out of character for her, and buoyed by the loving support of her family and friends she was soon back in class and busy with her normal activities.

After high school she enrolled at Cerritos Community College and graduated from the two-year program with an associate arts degree. She flirted with the idea of going on for an advanced degree, but she had already set her sights on continuing her success as a cheerleader and expanding her career as a professional model. Ultimately, she decided that continuing her formal education could wait. Her current career plans could not.

One early spring day in 1989 Linda drove to the Los Angeles Memorial Coliseum to try out for the Los Angeles Raiders cheerleading squad and was accepted as a Raiderette. Surviving the selection process was no mean feat. Hundreds of gorgeous young women showed up for the demanding auditions every year, sometimes as many as one thousand.

Linda's first test was surviving the "open call," when the number of performers was trimmed to a pool of about 150 finalists considered to have the kind of beauty, enthusiasm, athletic ability, and cheerleading experience the Raiders organization was looking for. Linda was among the approximate one-out-of-three who made the final cut and in May she was notified of her selection as one of the team's forty-nine Raiderettes. Aspiring Raiderettes had to be at least eighteen years old to audition, and the average age of the team's cheerleaders was twenty-five. Linda's age was smack in the middle. As a professional football cheerleader, she was in her prime.

Linda was also one of the few girls who earned most of her income as a professional model. Other cheerleaders came from a variety of professions including nursing and clerical work. All of the cheerleaders were high school graduates, more than half had college degrees, and several were still students. Although cheerleaders were paid by the Raiders, the amount wasn't enough to live on. Most of the Raiderettes, like Linda, performed for the mere fun and excitement. And it was fun!

Costumed in a crisply cute uniform of black and silver, the team colors, and armed with a pair of shiny pom-poms, Linda was a standout cheerleader from the very beginning. She was also one of the most popular cheerleaders approached by the squads of admiring men who crowded around them during breaks in the games, clamoring for autographs. Linda realized the adulation wouldn't last forever, and she counseled her friends to enjoy it while they could.

The cheerleaders didn't accompany the Raiders when the team flew to American Football Conference cities for out-of-town games. While the team was away, as well as when it was at home, Linda and her sister Raiderettes kept busy appearing at area charity, business, and promotional events. They entertained and visited with patients at veterans' hospitals, performed at benefits for the Special Olympics and youth groups, and they appeared at store openings and conventions. Regular cheerleading practices also demanded much of their time. Three times a week the Raiderettes traveled to a school in El Segundo, four miles north of Hermosa Beach, for exhausting three-hour practice sessions.

Being a Raiderette was a demanding job, but it had

its rewards. As an NFL cheerleader, Linda rubbed shoulders off the field with nationally known celebrities and other prominent movers and shakers in professions as diverse as sports, acting, business, and law. One night she might be a guest at a relatively sedate dinner and cocktails event sponsored by a big corporation. The next night she would be circulating through the crowd at a Super Bowl party hosted by a popular professional athlete such as basketball star Magic Johnson.

Cheerleading in the NFL is fiercely competitive, and just because a girl won a spot as a Raiderette during one particular year didn't mean she could remain on the squad the following season. Each season, the tryouts were held all over again and veteran cheerleaders found themselves competing with new, often much younger girls. Raiderettes signed one-year contracts and had to stay in peak physical condition to survive the cuts.

The contracts contained very specific rules governing the behavior of the cheerleaders who were so important to the image of the Raiders organization. According to the pacts, they were not permitted to date members of the team, and they were required to maintain a good public image for both the Raiders and for the Raiderettes. The cheerleaders were expressly prohibited from posing nude for any publications. Arrest for any felonies or damaging misdemeanor crimes were also grounds for dismissal.

With her wholesome blond beauty, and sleek, figure kept firm with regular workouts, Linda performed with the squad for five years and was featured as the cover girl on team calendars. In 1993, her final year with the squad, she was named "Raiderette of the Year."

Despite her success, she continued to show her usual appreciation and consideration for others. One of her best friends on the Raiderettes was a brunette who also modeled. Some other girls might have allowed the friendship to break up because of the pressures of sharing two such highly competitive jobs, but they turned their mutual interest into a positive experience. When Linda learned that an agent or a photographer needed a brunette, she recommended her friend. Her friend returned the favor whenever she heard about a shoot where a blonde was preferred.

Gretchen Stockdale, was another of Linda's close friends on the Raiderettes. Like Linda, Gretchen was a gorgeous blonde, who also modeled, including jobs posing in sexy lingerie. Gretchen posed for Victoria's Secret; Linda for Frederick's of Hollywood. Gretchen's main claim to fame so far, however, isn't tied to her work as a model. She became nationally known when it was revealed that on the night O. J. Simpson's ex-wife and her friend were slain the former football star telephoned her, apparently angling for a date. Although they didn't immediately go out together, he gave her his home number and Gretchen phoned him back several times after the slayings were reported on the news, leaving messages of support on his answering machine. According to Hollywood gossip, the pair became lovey-dovey for a while after Simpson's acquittal.

Linda's family ties were especially important to her. She was as close to her mother, from whom she got her middle name, as a mother and daughter could be. No matter what she was doing or where she was at—busy running between Raiderette practices and modeling gigs, in Southern California, or in San Francisco, New York, or some other city on a job—she never missed telephoning her mother at least once a day.

Her girlfriends sometimes kidded about the fidelity of the successful, busy young woman but they admired her for her devotion and continued close family ties. Linda talked with her friends during some of her business trips about the loving home her mother created for the Sobek family, and her hopes of eventually marrying and following in her footsteps.

In May 1995 she was twenty-six-years-old, and already a successful, self-confident woman who had made it in a demanding and extremely competitive profession, when she moved out of the cozy family home. Linda had left her parents' home before, but before her latest move into the house only a few yards from the pounding ocean surf in Hermosa Beach, she had always returned after becoming homesick.

Her bedroom in the blue-and-white house in Lakewood remained just as she left it, with stuffed animals, mementos from proms, and all the other collected treasures from her childhood and high school years, in place. Photos of the pride and joy of the Sobek family were also set up on shelves and hung on walls throughout the house. A large framed painting of Linda, created by artist Dennis Mukai, was hung in a special place of honor over the living room sofa. The tidy house was a virtual shrine to the couple's vibrantly gorgeous only daughter.

Linda's consideration for others extended beyond her family. After becoming a Raiderette, she never failed to send Mother's Day cards to Mary Barnes, who was the cheerleaders' coordinator. As a model, she never neglected writing thank-you notes, and the producers, editors, and photographers she worked with were used to receiving cards or letters with a few scribbled lines of appreciation from her after a shoot.

Her hectic schedule kept her on the run, but she didn't shortchange her spiritual life. Religion and personal faith were serious business to her, and she was a stickler about attending Sunday services, even when she was out of town posing for photographs or serving as hostess at a convention or trade show. Almost always, whenever she was temporarily parting with one of her friends, she left them with a cheery, "Good-bye and God bless."

Linda's signature farewell wasn't an empty statement. Early in 1995 she approached a girlfriend to talk over some problems in her life, and her chum and another childhood friend suggested she join the Baycities Community Church in Redondo Beach. Linda was raised as a Roman Catholic, but she began attending services at

Baycities—which was Baptist. She immediately began making new friends among the congregation and quickly became one of the most active young people in her new church. One of her special pleasures was joining other members of the spirited flock, enthusiastically singing hymns.

On her twenty-seventh birthday, the young woman was rebaptized and became a born-again Christian. The Reverend Jim Mackinga, pastor of her church, performed the ritual in the backyard pool of one of her friends in Torrance. Linda cried at the baptism.

The next day she also began keeping a diary, using it to record her most personal musings. Surprisingly, perhaps especially so because of the timing for beginning the journal, she didn't write about her church or her renewed spirituality. The blank pages were instead filled in with jottings about her desires, disappointments, difficulties with the young men in her life, and other self-doubts. Despite her uncommon beauty and *joie de vivre,* there were periods in her life when she hardly dated, or went out with men only sporadically. Neither she, nor Gretchen, her friend from the Raiderettes, had dates on Valentine's Day 1995 and the two beauties spent the evening together eating take-out food.

Entries in her diary were reserved for her private concerns and worries. Outwardly she was the same sweet girl who never failed to brighten up a room when she walked inside, or to provide the radiant, upbeat support for a friend who was having a bad day and needed a lift.

When Linda wasn't working or exercising, she was often reaching out to help others who were less fortunate than she was. She volunteered with the local Big Brother-Big Sister program, serving as a frequent companion for younger girls who were from broken families or otherwise in need of a role model. Her work with the volunteer group was fostered by her role as a Raiderette, but when she left the Raider organization she continued to help troubled girls.

Linda also kept up her membership in the California All-Pro Cheerleaders and performed with other girls at events for various charities and corporations. At other times she enjoyed quiet get-togethers with a friend, or simply turned up the stereo and spent private time listening to old Elvis Presley tunes, to Madonna, Rick Everett, or to Eddie Money. She was also an enthusiastic movie fan, and especially liked films featuring muscle man Arnold Schwarzenegger and action star Mel Gibson, or screen beauties Demi Moore and Kim Basinger.

An out-of-town freelance photographer who became one of her close male friends later told the *Breeze,* that he teased her about her attraction to the muscle men she met working out, and called them "steroid monkeys." Linda didn't mind. More ominously, the friend added that Linda could be too trusting at times. He twice spent the night with her because she insisted she didn't want him to rent a motel. The first night he was prepared to curl up on the couch, but Linda didn't have extra blankets so she invited him to sleep with her in her bed. Nothing happened that night, other than the two chums shared a good sleep. "She was totally trusting," he was quoted. "It was completely friendship."

When she left the Raiderettes after the 1993 season, only two years before the football team announced a move back to its old home city in Oakland, Linda put most of her professional energies into her modeling career. Although she was only twenty-five at that time she was already facing daunting competition in both professions from new girls who were often as much as five or more years younger than she.

Youthfulness is fleeting in the modeling world, and even the most beautiful women have found themselves suddenly no longer in demand for shoots. Models market their face, body, personal charisma, and their youth—or the illusion of youth. A few crow's-feet around the eyes, skin that has lost a bit of its youthful luster and elasticity, and the seemingly overnight flight of that special innocence and breathless look that only young girls have, and it can be all over. Linda knew it was time to work fulltime in the profession she had set her sights on since she was a teenager.

She was already firmly established locally as a body model, posing in scanty swimsuits, shorts, or sexy lingerie for calendars, catalogues, posters, and automotive magazines. The first time she modeled in a bikini for an automotive magazine, her picture appeared on the cover of the September 1989 issue of *Truckin'*. The magazine is published in Placentia in nearby Orange County for readers whose hobbies are customized and other fancy trucks.

In most of the jobs she did for the magazine over the years, she appeared by herself, or with a fellow male or female model, posing prettily in bikini or ragged cutoffs against a shiny new truck. On the large foldout cover of the January 1992 issue of *Truckin'*, however, she is shown in a bikini kneeling on a beach blanket next to a male model wearing a Santa Claus beard and wig, with shorts and a Hawaiian shirt. Three beautiful bikinied brunette models are gathered around them and a sleek new truck filled with Christmas gifts. Linda had found an important modeling niche. About once a year after her initial shoot for the magazine she appeared on the cover of *Truckin'* or its sister publication, *MiniTruckin'*.

She couldn't have been better located to take advantage of the career opportunities for her particular kind of modeling. Linda appeared in fetching swimsuit poses on calendars, as a magazine pinup girl, and she was booked as a hostess and model for national and international trade fairs and auto shows. She even posed as a poster girl for competing beers produced by two of the biggest breweries in the country, Budweiser and Coors.

She was also one of the most popular models for a locally produced cheesecake magazine, *Swimsuit Posters,* and for a sister publication, *Blast!* magazine. In various issues of *Swimsuit Posters,* she appeared as the cover girl, was featured on inside pages, and her picture appeared on foldout color pinups in the Malibu-based magazine. She first posed for the magazine in 1988 at Leo Carillo State Beach in Malibu after one of her modeling girlfriends tipped her off about the opportunity. It was the beginning of a long and rewarding association, and she posed at other sessions for the same publisher at a Hollywood studio, on Surfrider Beach in Malibu, Laguna Beach, and at her own backyard pool, in addition to other shoots. She posed off and on for the magazine before, during, and after she performed with the Raiderettes.

While she was a Raiderette and later, she made a habit of stopping by every so often to say hello to editors and photographers she had worked with to remind them she was still available for modeling jobs. Once Linda did a photo shoot with someone, they were likely to call on her again. Her personality and the seriousness with which she approached the job of modeling provided the perfect reinforcement and support for her striking good looks. On November 10, less than a week before she walked out of her house in Hermosa Beach for the last time, she pulled on a pretty yellow and blue striped bikini, slipped into a pair of white heels and worked another photo shoot for *Truckin'*. The shoot, by staff photographer Mike Shartsis, featured Linda posing with her long golden blond hair tumbling casually over her shoulders next to a customized "Full Effect CrewCab Ford." It was exactly the kind of job she had worked dozens of times before.

She never gave any serious consideration to the high-fashion world of runway modeling, or of trying to re-mold a career across the country in New York or other international fashion centers. She was close to her family in the South Bay, wasn't a clothes horse, was a few inches short, and her figure was too lush for her to find success among the anemic appearing, androgynous waifs who mince self-consciously down catwalks showing off designer clothes and seasonal new looks.

There was nothing androgynous or anemic-looking about Linda, and when the occasion called for it, such as enjoying a long, luxurious dinner over wine and cocktails with a boyfriend, she loved pulling out the stops, touching up with her favorite "Bijan" or "Giorgio," perfume, and dolling up in what she called her "cutesy outfits." There was always a good chance that would include a blouse or dress with polka dots. The romantic in her was attracted to roses, the color pink, a night of dancing, and tall, muscular men who were as athletically active and devoted to physical exercise and body building as she was. She loved sleek, powerful sports cars and talked dreamily to her friends about some day owning a Turbo Porsche 911. She also liked motorcycles.

Linda posed a few times with motorcycles for still shots and for a video showing her in a bikini, turning and swirling her hair around in a golden cloud. One of her favorite activities was pulling on a pair of shorts and a tube top then reveling in the joy and freedom of climbing onto a Harley-Davidson behind a boyfriend and holding on amid the thunder and the bellow of the powerful engine while they roared away. At other times she proudly paraded in beachside bikini contests and beauty shows. Linda looked her best in swimsuits, casual cutoffs, or tank tops and form-fitting blue jeans that showed off the firm swell of her breasts and the feminine flare of her hips.

She was devoted to keeping physically fit, and her regular workouts at Gold's Gym, other athletic clubs, and in the open air of the beach paid off with modeling assignments for muscle and fitness magazines. Linda was a regular along a section of the sandy shoreline of Venice Beach where handsome men and gloriously healthy looking women worked out pumping iron and sweating through carefully programmed routines of calisthenics.

Model Linda Sobek poses as a pert and pretty firefighter for an eye-catching pinup photo. (*Ramey Photo Agency*)

Linda Sobek in one of her classic cheesecake photos, showing off her beach-bunny blond beauty and charm. (*Ramey Photo Agency*)

A Los Angeles County Sheriff's Department helicopter lands on a road near a wash in the rugged San Gabriel mountains northeast of the city where a grave has been discovered. The makeshift grave is believed to hold the body of missing model Linda Sobek. (*AP/Wide World Photos*)

Robert Sobek waits with friends of his daughter Linda near a staging area as search-and-rescue teams move out to look for the missing woman in the San Gabriel Mountains. (*AP/Wide World Photos*)

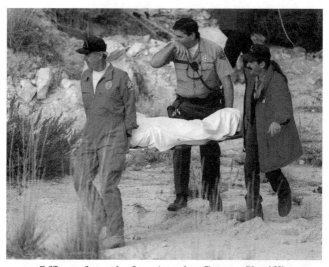

Officers from the Los Angeles County Sheriff's Department carry the body of a young blond woman toward a waiting van after the remains are unearthed from beneath a few inches of sand and gravel in a high peak area of the San Gabriel mountains. Photographer Charles Rathbun led searchers to the grave in a remote wash. (*AP/Wide World Photos*)

Flowers, wreaths, and modeling pictures of Linda Sobek are placed on the front steps of her home in Hermosa Beach by grieving friends. (*AP/Wide World Photos*)

The slain model's parents, Robert Sobek (left) and Elaine Sobek (right foreground) flank their only daughter's casket as it is loaded into a white hearse following her funeral service at the First Baptist Church of Lakewood in Long Beach. (*AP/Wide World Photos*)

Mourners bid farewell to Linda Sobek as 100 white doves are released in front of the First Baptist Church at the conclusion of her funeral service. (*AP/Wide World Photos*)

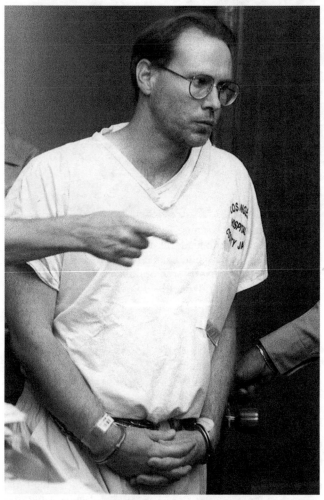

A dour and shackled Charles Edgar Rathbun being led into
Municipal Court in Torrance, California, where he pleaded
innocent to the murder of Linda Sobek.
(*AP/Wide World Photos*)

The home of automotive and cheesecake photographer Charles Rathbun in the 1900 block of Canyon Drive in Hollywood. (*Courtesy of Coll Metcalfe*)

The house in Hermosa Beach that Linda Sobek shared with three roommates before her mysterious disappearance. (*Courtesy of Coll Metcalfe*)

One of the last photos taken of model and former Los Angeles Raiders cheerleader Linda Elaine Sobek. The picture appeared on thousands of flyers circulated throughout the Santa Monica South Bay area by her friends seeking information on her whereabouts after she vanished.
(AP/Wide World Photos)

So many physical fitness buffs flocked to the stretch of sand that locals referred to it as "Muscle Beach." While a few regulars or casual visitors among the clowns, jugglers, skaters, panhandlers, and strollers watched from the busy walkway, Linda and her male and female companions primped, pumped iron, and grunted through their arduous outdoor workouts.

Linda made a habit of working out one hour a day, six days a week either on the beach or in the gym. She organized her fitness schedule with meticulous care, devoting thirty-minutes of each workout to her upper body, and the other thirty-minutes to her lower body—especially her legs. She did leg curls, leg extensions, calf-raises, squats, and lunges. Weight lifting was an important part of the total workout.

In June 1995 Linda was one of seven fit and healthy women from Muscle Beach featured with full-page photos in *Muscle & Fitness* magazine. Linda's picture shows her in a skimpy one-piece outfit with the tummy area exposed, holding a pair of inline skates. She was quoted saying that being "genetically gifted" wasn't good enough for her. "There's a big difference between a slender girl who looks nice," she said, "and a girl who works out to take her body to the next level."

The workouts, careful food selection, and avoidance of tobacco or excess alcohol all contributed to maintaining a slender twenty-four-inch waist and trim 103 to 110 pounds on her carefully toned and sun-bronzed five foot four inch frame. She loved Chinese food, Mexican food, sushi, chicken salad, chocolate-chip cookies, and ice cream, but was careful to eat it in small amounts and any excess calories were quickly burned off in workouts. Even with the benefit of the workouts, indulging herself with favorite treats wasn't an everyday event. Most often when she was eating out she dined in health food restaurants. Her body was too important to her to risk damaging it with bad habits.

In 1995 she turned to another fast-growing segment

of the beauty and fitness business and was featured in a
workout video performing aerobics. Linda was shown
on the film produced by Brentwood Home Video, working up a sweat performing everything from push-ups and
squats to lunges and leg bends.

A woman as popular as Linda could make a good
living as a model, although she didn't earn anything near
the fees available to international fashion goddesses like
Elle MacPherson, Germany's Claudia Schiffer, or Dutch
beauty Karen Mulder. Their earnings can top fifty thousand dollars on a good day. Today's supermodels are
supercelebrities who form their own marketing companies, promote their names and images with a host of
products from cosmetics and clothes to little girls' toys,
and frequently make the transition to film star. Slick
magazines follow them on location, reveal their beauty
secrets, film their weddings, and profile their lives and
careers.

Fashion queens Schiffer, Mulder, and Naomi Camp-
bell appeared together in Paris early in 1996 with dolls
fashioned in their likeness and destined for the toy
stores. Claudia has starred in an entire series of exercise
tapes, focusing on the abs, the buns, the arms, and the
legs.

Former *Charlie's Angels* Farrah Fawcett and Jaclyn
Smith, along with beauties Lauren Hutton, Sharon
Stone, Cindy Crawford, and Jessica Lange are a few of
the big-time models who have made the transition to
Hollywood film star. A television series, *Models, Inc.*,
has also been produced starring Kylie Travis as the her-
oine.

Linda hadn't achieved that kind of success, but she
was busily expanding her professional horizons and
looking forward to a future as an agent or actress. Like
her colleagues in the business who concentrated on body
modeling, Linda was usually paid between one hundred
dollars and two hundred dollars a day for her work. It
depended on the job and the client. But some days she

had more than one assignment, and she was also able to occasionally double her pay when a photographer was shooting a couple of assignments at once. If she posed for both jobs, she was paid separately for each.

Her income from modeling would never make her rich, but she wasn't forced to pinch pennies. Hollywood is obsessed with the illusion of youth and beauty, and modeling is big business among publishers, advertising agencies, and other closely related industries throughout the Los Angeles area. Advertisements and write-ups in professional publications, daily newspapers, and on the electronic media promote auditions and screenings for experienced and aspiring models every day. Children, handsome men, and senior citizens of every race and age are invited to enter a glamorous profession that could make them rich and famous. But the opportunities are especially enticing for beautiful young women.

Hardly anyone in the trade worked every day, however. Models are freelancers, and they have to scramble for jobs in the fast-lane profession. Linda was one of the most successful and worked more often than most.

Details about exactly when and how Linda met the temperamental photographer from Columbus are hazy, but it seems possible that their initial meeting may have occurred at one of the popular auto shows in the Los Angeles area. She also may have been recommended by one of her modeling friends, or someone else involved in some other facet of the business.

Like most professional models, Linda was used to working through an agency. She worked with Patty Brand for more than three years, and many or most of her jobs were booked through the agency during that time. Occasionally a photographer or an executive with some advertising agency, business, or convention promoter would telephone and she would make her own arrangements. By 1995 she was doing many of her own bookings, as well as managing fifteen other models. It is not unusual for a model to move into managing or agenting after gaining experience, and Linda had the intelligence, imagination, organizational ability, and contacts to find new success in that phase of the business.

When agents send a model out on a job they are expected to know all the details. They know where the shoot will be conducted; the identity and reputation of the photographer and other people expected to be present; how the model is to be clothed, or unclothed; and when the job is scheduled to begin and when it is expected to end.

Models check in by telephone with their agencies, often as soon as they arrive at the site of a shoot, and before they leave. New jobs sometimes crop up on the spur of the moment, and when that happens checking in with an agent can lead to added income. But sticking with the system is most vital for safety considerations. When young women with the kind of sparkling beauty Linda possessed climb into a car and drive off with a stranger or a casual acquaintance it's merely playing it smart to make sure ahead of time that someone else knows who she's with and where they are going.

Linda was an experienced model and she knew about the perils and pitfalls lurking in the background that form the dark side of the business. Normally she was cautious as could be, but there were times when her gentle nature took over and she could be artless and overly trusting. For at least once, it seems, she took a chance and violated the safety rules that she was known to abide by for herself and for the other women whom she worked with. It was a miscalculation that may have cost the quintessential California girl her life.

SEVEN

A Forest Grave

Rathbun and his lawyer spent the remainder of Wednesday night with police searching for the crude grave he scratched out in the forest floor for the model. Shortly after 9 P.M. they were seated in a county sheriff's car and driven away from the Hollywood station, into the mountains to conduct the search. It was a fruitless exercise.

Rathbun recalled that he had scraped the grave out of the sand and gravel somewhere along a side road off the Angeles Crest Highway. It was difficult to pinpoint exactly, but he directed them into the foothills north of the national forest above La Canada-Flintridge.

The photographer's confusion may have been understandable. It's easy for anyone to lose their bearings in the wilderness, and even experienced mountaineers have been known to become lost in broad daylight. So it seemed possible that a man dealing with such a traumatic event as the terrible accident he said cost the model her life could become confused and have trouble retracing his steps. That was especially true when the forest was shrouded in night shadows.

Tall trees, boulder-dappled mountains, sheer cliffs, treacherous switchbacks, and bone-dry lake beds don't make very good landmarks during the day or at night when hundreds or thousands of others that look just like them are scattered all over the place. Rathbun couldn't find the dry patch of sand and gravel where he said he had buried the body.

Sometime around 5:30 Thanksgiving morning, the homicide detectives had enough. They called off the search—for the time being. Shortly before the small caravan of cars headed back to the Hollywood station, they pulled into the lot of a convenience store and parked so they could pick up coffee and snacks. Over the mountain ridges to the east, the first slender fingers of orange and yellow light from the approaching dawn were just beginning to claw their way through the darkness.

Saldana and Nichols were talking outside the store about the investigation and the search, when the lawyer expressed displeasure over the questioning of Rathbun outside his presence. He asked if his client was read his Miranda rights. Saldana replied that he wasn't. According to the lawyer's later recollections, Saldana then added that Nichols should know that any information gathered from Rathbun before he was read the warning couldn't be used against him in court. A few minutes later everyone climbed back into the car to complete the return to the urban sprawl below.

Rathbun didn't remain at the Hollywood station very long, and just about the time morning rush hour traffic was beginning to clog the intimidating cross-stitch of freeways and city streets, he was loaded back into a sheriff's car and driven to the HBPD. When the dusty car pulled up and parked next to the headquarters Rathbun was led inside, his handcuffs were removed, and he was locked in a holding cell under a close suicide watch. Almost immediately the physically and emotionally exhausted suspect curled up on his bunk and fell into an uneasy sleep.

Detective Bice figured Rathbun had shared all the information he was going to give to them. So while he was catching some shut-eye, she began planning and organizing a more broad-ranging search to be carried out the next day without him. The Mill Creek Ranger Station was designated as the command post.

Beginning at about 5 P.M. on Thanksgiving Day, a three-man squad from the Antelope Valley Search and Rescue Team headed by Sergeant Mike Becker, roamed through a canyon near the intersection of Big Rock Creek Road and Big Pines Highway for four hours. They found a woman's compact and signs of blood. By 9 P.M. they were forced by darkness to call off the effort until Friday.

The compact and blood were quicky ruled out as evidence in the case. They apparently had nothing to do with the missing woman and were merely an example of the curious grab bag of material collected from the forest throughout the several days of the spotty search by professionals and by Linda's personal friends. Some of the items were exceedingly interesting and had the early appearance of potential clues, but were ultimately eliminated as possible evidence.

They included a backpack and a wet suit about the right size to fit a woman of Linda's build. They were found while Rathbun was being questioned at the Hollywood Division Station, and he was asked if they were hers. The photographer was as puzzled by the strange discovery as everyone else. Linda didn't take anything like that along on the photo shoot, he assured his interrogators.

Earlier on Thanksgiving Day after Nichols had also caught a few hours of badly needed sleep and had a meal, the lawyer drove to the Hermosa Beach jail with Rathbun's glasses and a change of clothes. Jailers didn't permit him to give the clothing to his client, but he was allowed to speak privately with him for about fifteen or twenty minutes.

After the brief meeting, Nichols jotted down a note on one of his business cards instructing Rathbun not to speak to anyone about the case unless he had a lawyer with him. Nichols asked a jail matron to give the card to his client, but she told him she wasn't permitted to do that. She did agree to place it with the inmate's personal clothing which investigators had inventoried and stored.

Nichols was determined not to take any chances that his client would be questioned again without a lawyer present, so he jotted messages down on the last two business cards he had with him, and also gave them to the matron. One of the cards was directed to Lieutenant Wright, and the other to Detectives Saldana and Thomas Thompson, who both participated in the search. Nichols asked her to pass them on for him. The hand-jotted messages on both cards warned that his client was not to be questioned or taken anywhere unless a defense attorney was present.

The first card read: "To Lt. Wright: Charles Rathbun has a desire to fully and completely cooperate with the police. However, he has been instructed not to make any statements or go on any trips without his attorney. He will soon be represented by the Public Defender's Office or a criminal atty, which I am not. I trust you understand." Nichols concluded the cramped note by adding his unlisted home telephone number.

The other note read: "To Raul Saldana . . . Tom Thompson: I appreciate the professionalism you have demonstrated to date. Charlie's attitude is one of complete cooperation but he has been instructed not to give any statements outside the presence of counsel. Thank you for honoring this." Again, he concluded by jotting down his home telephone number.

Thanksgiving Day brought bad news for Rathbun's friend, Shannon Meyer. She was suspended from her job as a reserve deputy until a more comprehensive look by the Sheriff's Department's Internal Affairs Division could be taken into her involvement with the case. Subsequently, Meyer was reinstated to full duty.

In Lakewood a few miles inland, the missing model's mother, along with relatives and friends, spent a bleak holiday gathered together in the house in the 11000 block of 205th Street, plunged deeply into the darkness of their dreadful anxieties. Linda's father was absent from the somber gathering most of the day. He was with friends and other relatives, combing through the national forest in the increasingly desperate search for his daughter. A force of about forty civilians and volunteer police officers began combing the national forest for traces of her on Tuesday, and continued working through the holiday. Off-duty Buena Park Policeman John Vredenburgh was among the loyal band of family friends who showed up to spend Thanksgiving Day roaming the vast forest.

At about 7:30 Friday morning Rathbun cut his wrists with a disposable Bic razor blade. Jailers were just outside the cell but the prisoner managed to make two shallow slashes in each wrist and use his own blood to scrawl a scarlet apology on one of the walls before they could rush inside and wrestle the razor away from him. The grisly message indicated he didn't mean to hurt anyone. His bunk and the sink in the austerely furnished cubicle were also splashed with thick streaks and puddles of blood.

Even though Rathbun had threatened to kill himself and was being closely watched because he was considered to be a suicide risk, guards decided it was safe to give him the razor because he seemed to be in good spirits when he awakened Friday morning. The prisoner was anxious to freshen up and shave before dealing with the anticipated pressures of the new day.

Paramedics administered first aid and drove Rathbun to the South Bay Medical Center in Redondo Beach where the superficial cuts in his wrists were stitched, then bandaged in the emergency room. Despite the large amount of blood smeared in the cell, if the wrist slashing was indeed an effort to commit suicide, it seemed to be a feeble attempt. A blood sample was also taken from the injured prisoner by a member of the hospital staff after Rathbun consented to a request from Detective Saldana.

While Rathbun was being patched up, Lieutenant Wright was at the ranger station designated as the staging area for the search, and he instructed a sergeant to telephone the hospital to find out if Rathbun would agree to help look for the model. The sergeant passed the message on to Saldana, who talked with Rathbun. The prisoner said he was willing to help, if it was okay with his lawyer.

At about 10:30 A.M., after the rumpled photographer was patched up, he was led from the clinic with his head down, his bandaged wrists carefully cuffed in front of him, and the right breast pocket and sleeve of his white shirt splattered with his own blood. Reporters and photographers watched, shouted questions that went unanswered, and snapped pictures.

While waiting for a Los Angeles County Sheriff's Department helicopter to resume the search with a group of detectives for the body of the missing model, Rathbun volunteered some information to Saldana, the detective later claimed. "I put a rock on her to mark the spot," he blurted out. "Mark the spot?" the detective said he responded in surprise. "I put a rock on her so the animals wouldn't carry her away," Rathbun said.

Saldana said he played it cautious. He let the matter drop and didn't push for more information at that time beyond the tantalizing scrap that was volunteered.

The manacled prisoner was helped into the helicopter, then flown to the ranger station and led into a small room off the main operations area to wait while senior officers continued preparations to resume the search. Lieutenant Wright assigned HBPD Detective Dean R. Menart to stay in the room and keep a close watch on Rathbun to make sure there were no further suicide attempts. The two men chatted about photography, the mountains, and exchanged other small talk, but according to Menart's later statements, he was careful to keep the conversation away from anything relating to the search or the overall investigation.

While Rathbun was cooling his heels at the ranger station, Nichols was home with his television set turned to the local news. He was stunned when an announcer reported that a suspect in the death of the model from Hermosa Beach had slashed his wrists earlier that morning in his jail cell. The suspect was not critically injured and was patched up at the medical center, the announcer added.

According to legal documents later filed in the courts, Nichols telephoned the Sheriff's Department and told homicide detective Michal Bumcrot he was an attorney representing Rathbun. His client wished to help authorities find the body of the missing woman, and that was agreeable to the lawyer. But Nichols reportedly said he himself didn't wish to participate in the search.

Bumcrot telephoned the HBPD to notify investigators there about the promising new development. Nichols had barely hung up and turned back to digesting the fast-breaking news when the telephone rang again. It was Saldana. Calling from his car phone, the homicide sleuth confirmed the news report and urged the lawyer to join in the renewed hunt for the body. Saldana told the lawyer he would be picked up at his home by car and driven to the Angeles Crest Highway. Before the car reached the lawyer's house, however, Lieutenant Wright telephoned.

According to the officer's later court statement, he told the lawyer he understood Nichols had consented to allow his client to help look for Linda. Nichols confirmed the agreement, but stressed that he wanted it understood his client was only to help in the search and was not supposed to answer any questions about the woman's death.

Wright said he understood and recommended that Nichols join them at the ranger station so he could accompany his client. Then Wright arranged for a Sheriff's

Department helicopter to meet the lawyer at the Holly-wood-Burbank Airport and ferry him into the mountains. Early in the afternoon Nichols walked into the ranger station. When he asked to see his client, he was directed to Rathbun's room and they had a short, hurried, private conversation.

Nichols was a good lawyer who knew his business. But his business was litigating medical malpractice suits. This maelstrom of shooting, jail cells, interrogations, late-night searches along darkened forest roads, and helicopter sweeps over the Angeles wilderness that he was caught up in was a whole new, confusing, and troubling experience. The events transpiring around him were traveling at warp speed. Everywhere he turned there were more cops; they were coming out of the woodwork. And none of them showed any inclination to back off for a few moments, so he could take a deep breath and sit down for a quiet moment and figure things out.

Although he should have been recognized as an important, although reluctant, player in the drama, no one was paying much attention to his advice. It seemed he was being treated more as a somewhat privileged onlooker than as legal counsel to the suspect. The harried civil lawyer told his client not to talk to anyone, and his client talked. He told police not to talk to his client, and they talked to him anyway. They didn't even pay any serious attention to him when he tried to recuse himself from the case and said he wanted out so the job of defending the murder suspect could be turned over to a criminal defense attorney.

A day and a half after Nichols's unsuccessful efforts to bow out of the mess as gracefully as he could, he and the freelance photographer were led to a huge Sheriff's Department helicopter waiting nearby. While dozens of police officers, some in uniform, others in plain clothes, stood about preparing to begin the ground portion of the search, the furiously spinning rotors of the Sikorsky were kicking up a noisy roar of dust and debris. Rathbun and Nichols ducked their heads, as people tend to do even when the rotors are high above them, and climbed into the chopper with Wright, another officer, and the pilot to look for the grave.

A few minutes earlier, the suspected killer had poured over a stack of maps of the forest that were spread out for him at the station. He carefully studied the lines, squiggles, landmark logos, and place names initially drawn on paper with the aim of helping travelers find their way in the dense wilderness. Despite his meticulous inspection of the maps, when Rathbun and his escort resumed the search in earnest, he appeared to be still confused over the location.

The handcuffed man had talked during his interrogation at the Hollywood Division Station about leaving the model in a sandy desert area. But he was directing the pilot to heavily wooded mountainsides of the vast forest where the trees and underbrush were so thick and such a deep green that in the distance they took on a purple hue. It was the kind of wildly primeval terrain that a Daniel Boone, Jim Bridger, or a Grizzly Adams would have felt right at home in.

While Rathbun was hovering over the wilderness in a helicopter, criss-crossing an area of mountains and broad patches of scrub desert that were as desolate and bleak as moonscape, search and rescue teams on the ground were spreading out and taking their own carefully organized look around the wilderness. Most of them, including sheriff's deputies, civilian volunteers, and a mountain patrol, had been on the job since 7 A.M.

Members of the Montrose, Sierra Madre, and the Altadena search and rescue teams were broken up into smaller units and assigned specific areas to explore. Most of the units were composed of a single deputy or volunteer, but a few were formed of two or three, and five people were assigned to the Monte Cristo Campground and creek beds—the general area where the remains of Kimberly Pandelios were recovered years earlier.

The largest group was headed by Becker, who returned to the canyons and campground near the site of the earlier search with an expanded team of sixteen deputies and civilian volunteers. Four members of the team were mounted on horses. Some of the searchers were sent off to check inside ramshackle abandoned mines, and others concentrated on roadsides, and still more camping areas including the Chilao and Pacifico Campgrounds.

Several K-9 units were also assembled, and under the direction of a sergeant they concentrated their search on the Monte Cristo Campground and along the Santa Clara Divide Road. The dogs selected for that particular search were bloodhounds that follow ground scent, as opposed to air sniffing dogs such as Alsatians. As their name implies the sad-looking, wrinkled hounds were excellently equipped to pick up blood trails with their sensitive noses.

Linda's friends also resumed their own desperate efforts to find her. Despite the dispiriting news originating with Rathburn that she was dead, some of the determined young people weren't yet willing to give up and admit that she might not be alive somewhere—perhaps badly injured, but still with a spark of life in her.

Others, who were more practical, or simply more discouraged, accepted the sad fact that she was dead. But they also wanted her back, even if the only thing they could do after recovering her remains was to give her a proper burial. They gathered along with Linda's more stubbornly optimistic friends near the staging site at the ranger station to organize their own search teams, or expectantly wait for reports on the progress of the operation while their worst fears continued to congeal and form into ugly clots of despair.

Sipping cups of hot black coffee in the morning and cans of cool diet soda pop or unsweetened iced tea in the afternoon, about thirty men and women clustered among a fleet of parked pickup trucks and off-road vehicles much like those that Linda made her living posing with. They perched on the tops of truck cabs, balanced precariously on tailgates, or stood with their hands in their pockets listening to the tinny crackle of police radios and faint reports on commercial stations that faded in and out in the high mountain elevation while tracing the progress of the search.

The sad vigil attracted muscular men along with slender young women who almost uniformly wore their long hair over their shoulders like Linda did. An uncommon number of women among the group were uncommonly pretty and blond. But the trademark smiles of Linda's model pals were missing and their faces were creased with concern. They weren't there to pose for glamorous photo shoots or for a beauty contest, but for a depressingly serious last-gasp effort to find their missing chum.

The special bond that united the models and their husbands or boyfriends were closely tied to the profession that so many of the women shared. There was a keen sense of sisterhood among the models and cheerleaders that transcended petty professional and personal rivalries, and was far more genuine and caring than the superficiality of insincere kisses, hugs, and coos that so often marked greetings or temporary good-byes.

The dress for the day tended to be khaki or denim; simple tops or light jackets for the women, and plaid or chambray shirts for the men. Almost everyone wore practical, solid shoes, the kind that hold up on long walks along primitive mountain roads or footpaths or while clutching at scrub brush and digging toes into tiny ledges while scrambling up and down the precipitous rock-strewn sides of forbidding ravines.

Linda's sixty-two-year-old father pulled on a baseball cap and sunglasses, then joined her young friends at the staging area, looking grave and dignified while he listened to the crackling of the radios. After the helicopter lifted off with Rathbun inside, the anguished parent broke into tears while trying to thank his daughter's many friends who had rallied at the site in support. He said he hoped "this turkey" would at last lead authorities to his daughter.

Some of Linda's friends doubted that was going to happen, pointing to the unsuccessful foray into the mountains the previous Wednesday. How could the photographer experience the ghastly trauma of accidentally killing someone, burying them, and then forget where they were at, they asked.

Early Friday afternoon the same psychic who told Linda's friends about the parked car, walked through the house the missing model had shared in Hermosa Beach with her roommates. The psychic said the vibrations she picked up indicated there was still a good chance the girl was alive, but they had to get to her as soon as possible. A clairvoyant, who works through images that flash in her mind or before her eyes, the psychic said she saw Linda facing a red brick wall. ". . . she's looking at a red brick wall."

Some of Linda's friends chartered a helicopter, and late Friday afternoon Gene Smith, the psychic, and two other passengers lifted off with the pilot and headed for the forest. Linda could be alive somewhere out there, wandering around frightened, hurt, and lost. They carried a supply of drinking water and a warm jacket along for her, in case she was thirsty and cold, or in shock.

Kelly Flynn's brother, Jeff Flynn, who was Linda's lone male roommate, saw them off at Torrance Municipal Airport, but he didn't join the flight because he simply couldn't share their irrepressible optimism. Their positive attitude showed in their eyes, he told a reporter for the Torrance newspaper. "I'm not as positive; I'm a realist . . ." he added. "This whole thing, since it began, it's been sucking everything out of me." Flynn first met Linda through mutual friends eight years earlier, and they became especially close while working out together at Gold's Gym in Redondo Beach.

The helicopter carrying the psychic and Linda's friends joined a small fleet of other helicopters, including some from the media, that were swooping low over the side roads, gullies, and washes in some of the more remote areas of the forest. Television news crews broadcast descriptions of the search live from the air and from the ground.

The search and rescue crews on the ground crisscrossed hundreds of acres of forest and highway in the mountains throughout the long, arduous afternoon. After crossing off the scrabbly desert area near Palmdale and eliminating the summit area near the Valyermo Ranger District, the ground teams along with searchers scanning from the air, concentrated on other equally harsh but hillier areas around the Mill Creek Summit. An area of primeval wilderness, filled with dense forest and underbrush, interspersed with rocky cliffs and thorny washes and ravines, it was about ten-to-twelve miles as the crow—or the helicopter flies—from Big Tujunga Canyon.

The last brilliant rays of the late autumn sun were gleaming in the distance over the Pacific when Wright pointed out to the suspect that the light was almost gone and Linda's chances of surviving another night were almost nil if she was still alive somewhere down on the forest floor. It was about 4 P.M. It seemed to the police lieutenant that Rathbun was more interested in the view from the helicopter and the media coverage than he was in finding the woman they were looking for.

Then, just minutes before sunset, Rathbun pointed to a gravelly wash that was shaped like an arrowhead and jutted just off the Mount Pacifico Road in a high peak area of the San Gabriels. He said he thought that was where he buried the model. A short retainer wall was constructed along the side of the wash, separating the flat dirt surface of the isolated clearing from a sheer drop-off.

The pilot set the helicopter down on the cleared area, kicking up a thick skurry of dust with the furiously churning rotor blades. Three men jumped out, and ignoring the shower of grit that dug into their faces, hurried toward a hump of soft dirt near the retaining wall. They took a quick look, then one of them turned and gave a "thumbs-up" sign to the passengers still in the helicopter. The pilot radioed the ground searchers that they had found the body.

The site was about fifteen miles west and upmountain from the desert area near the small town of Palmdale that was scoured earlier in the day from the ground. It was on the north side of the San Gabriels, that separate the urban sprawl of the Los Angeles Basin from the parched Mojave Desert. And like the psychic had said, Linda was next to a wall. The rough cinder block structure stretched along a drainage culvert for about twenty feet, and a lumpy covering of red dust and sand gave it a scarlet tinge.

Within a few minutes, a caravan of ground vehicles streamed into the wash and stern-faced men and women began climbing out and assembling at the end of the narrow, bumpy dirt lane leading to the clearing. The ominous mound of dirt and rocks was piled up only a few feet away. When one of the officers lifted a heavy slab of granite from the top of the pile, a glimpse of a human knee was exposed in the pebbly grave.

Detective Bice was one of the first officers to reach the scene, and she squatted over the grave to scoop away a thin film of sand until she uncovered a flash of skin to further confirm a body was buried there. A few strands of long, golden blond hair, stiff with grime, were just below the dusty sprinkle of dirt at the top.

Ironically, Cosby and some of his colleagues were planning to move their search to the Santa Clara Divide Road and the Mount Pacifico area when news reporters stopped him and said the body had been found. The grave was also in the same general area scouted earlier in the day by almost two-dozen officers and volunteers, including a unit from the Montrose search and rescue team. Even though they were backed up by bloodhounds the early effort was unsuccessful. The terrain was especially rugged, with huge trees, enormous boulders, brush-clogged ravines, sheer drop-offs, and litters of impassable chaparral that was as sticky as molasses and as sharp as barbwire. The rough topography offered thousands of potential hiding places for a body.

The early-evening forest darkness was swiftly closing in and search leaders concerned about contaminating or destroying possible evidence in the faint light, called off activities in the clearing until the following morning. The job of exhuming the body would be the responsibility of trained investigators with the Los Angeles County Coroner's Department and of forensic anthropologists.

The group of officers knew the importance of maintaining the integrity of the crime scene. And they were aware that the care and abilities of the technicians combing through and processing the immediate area for evidence was critical. If they weren't up to snuff or didn't do their jobs exactly right, when a case moved into the courts, defense attorneys could romp.

Working quickly and efficiently, police marked off the site of the primitive grave with bright orange crime scene tape. Then a couple of officers were assigned to remain at the gravesite and trade off guarding it through the night. A few minutes later, all but one of the vehicles turned around and began the long twenty-five-mile drive down the narrow mountain roads toward the lowland highways and city streets of Los Angeles and its suburbs that were already blinking with lights and radiating in the distance like luminescent streamers.

The murder suspect never left the helicopter at the crime scene. He was ferried back to Los Angeles and taken to the Men's Central Jail, where he was booked on preliminary charges of homicide.

Authorities had found a body, but because of the rush of darkness they hadn't been able to remove it from the crude grave or determine with certainty that it was the remains of the young woman they were looking for. They didn't even know for certain if it was the body of a male or female. The implication that the search for Linda Sobek was over, was unavoidable, however. The man who told police he accidentally killed the model, then buried her in the remote mountain wash, had led them to the shallow grave. It was only four miles south of Mill Creek Summit and the ranger station used to coordinate the search. A Sheriff's Department spokesman later told reporters that the body was so well concealed in the out-of-the-way area of the forest that it may never have been found without Rathbun's help.

Early that evening, a police representative drove to the Sobek home in Lakewood where the family had kept a fearful watch throughout the day waiting for word of their daughter, to relay the dreadful news that a body was found.

Linda's friends already knew the bad news. Those who were standing vigil at the ranger station heard the depressing report on the crackling police radios, and their final hopes were dashed. Her roommates were stationed in front of the television throughout most of the dismally suspenseful afternoon watching, fearful and subdued while events unfolded and were broadcast by crews accompanying the search teams. A single lighted candle was placed on a table behind them, next to a stack of "missing" flyers that were no longer needed.

In Lakewood, Wayne Willette, who was retained as the family attorney, told inquiring news reporters that the Sobeks had no immediate comment. Linda's parents and brother were enduring "extreme bereavement," he said.

Earlier Mrs. Sobek talked briefly by phone with a reporter for *The Daily News of Los Angeles,* and in a voice choking with emotion, said of Linda: "Everybody should be lucky and have a daughter like that."

About an hour after daybreak the next day police returned to the forest wash with a select team of experts to begin carefully exhuming the body from the grave. It was almost exactly 7 A.M. when homicide detectives, coroners investigators, and a forensic anthropologist began their grim work. A blue canopy was suspended over the gravesite on four poles about ten feet high to shield it from camera crews in media helicopters, and to provide some protection from the sun for the workers. A meticulous inspection of the immediate area was also begun by other officers and technicians for possible evidence before the shallow mound of earth and stone was touched by the exhumation team.

The grave was measured, and crime scene technicians also utilized the few objects in the immediate area capable of serving as landmarks to triangulate distances from the gently sloping mound. Photographs were taken of the grave and of the immediate surroundings, plaster cast impressions were made of tire tracks on the dirt and gravel floor of the turnout, and the entire area was again meticulously combed for even the tiniest bit of trash. Anything from a beer can to a cigarette butt, a swatch of cloth or a chunk of rock with a suspicious rusty stain on it could be a potential clue. Everything that was found was photographed where it was first observed, then collected, placed in bags, and marked with the date, location, name of the detective or technician, and sealed inside.

When the exhumation team at last began their grim task, they didn't merely begin to dig away the dirt and stones, then lift the body out. Every precaution was taken to preserve possible evidence in and around the grave. They removed the earth and debris a bit at a time, making close visual examinations of every chunk or slab of granite piled on top of the grave, then meticulously sifted through the sand and dirt as it was lifted away from the body.

A forensic photographer snapped still pictures, recording every step of the operation, while his colleagues used their plastic gloved hands and the tips of shovels or trowels to expose the dirt grimed corpse of a once-beautiful young blond woman lying faceup a few inches under the gravel, sand, and rocks. The remains of the young woman in the grave were still clad in the same top and pair of shorts over a white unitard she was wearing when she walked out of the gym in Redondo Beach.

It was hot, sticky, and still in the forest, without so much as a faint breeze, and the sun rapidly burned away the last traces of early-morning ground mist and dew. While the small assemblage of men and women worked, the underarms, waists, and collars on the brown Sheriff's Department uniforms and the blue jumpsuits worn by coroner's employes quickly soaked through with sweat.

It was a few minutes after 3 P.M. when the body was at last lifted onto a red canvas stretcher, covered with a white sheet, and loaded into a van. It was driven in the van to another larger flat area a short distance away and transferred to a waiting Sheriff's Department helicopter. The entire exhumation process had taken slightly more than eight hours.

Minutes later the chopper lifted off and began the noisy flight to the urban clutter below, finally landing at the Los Angeles County-USC Medical Center in the heart of downtown Los Angeles. It was transferred there to another van and driven a short distance to the adjoining office of the county medical examiner and morgue.

At about six o'clock that evening a color Polaroid picture taken of the face of the woman pulled from the grave was shown to some of Linda's friends at the Lakewood Sheriff's Station, and they sadly confirmed it was the model. Her parents couldn't bear to look at the pictures and chose to hang onto their memories of her as she was when she was alive. Willette told the media the

Sobeks were trying to remain strong. "Obviously," he said, "there's a lot of grief."

The forty-five-year-old attorney added Linda's family was hopeful that the photographer's story of how she died would stand up because they didn't want to think of her having gone through an ordeal of fear and suffering. "If her death was brought upon by a vehicle," he said, "that's better than some ways of going."

Friends and relatives continued to flock to the house throughout the weekend, and Linda's minister stopped by on Saturday to drop off a video tape of her baptism a few weeks earlier. The grieving family watched the video and shared other fond memories of Linda during much of the afternoon.

Earlier in the day, Linda's father left the house on 205th Street with two of her friends from the Raiderettes and approached a group of reporters standing around and talking with each other or seated in folding chairs and scanning local newspapers. Everyone was still waiting for the formal announcement that the remains were positively identified as those of the missing model. The grieving father and his daughter's friends passed out bagels and cream cheese from two paper plates to the unusually subdued news hawks.

The retired Rockwell International Corporation engineer doted on his sparkling daughter, and he was showing the strain from the calamity that had struck at the heart of his family. His eyes were tired and sunken from lying awake too many nights listening hopefully for what he described as the "clippity-clop" of her high heels outside on the driveway. He had trouble sleeping, and even when he did manage to drop off into an exhausted slumber he awakened again whenever a car door slammed outside, desperately hoping it would be Linda. It never was.

"God wanted her at this time," and the people who loved Linda needed to put aside their selfish desires and accept that the Creator has greater plans, he said of his daughter. "God wanted her more than us."

The polite, spiritual man didn't have anything to say to the crowd of reporters about the presumed guilt or innocence of the photographer who had already admitted responsibility for Linda's death. But the heartbroken father had some advice for other young women with stars in their eyes and dreams of modeling careers.

"Beware, be careful out there. Don't go alone," he cautioned. "You can see what happened."

Kimiko Tanaka, a model and Raiderette who was one of Linda's closest friends, echoed the warning about photo shoots in private locations or isolated areas. "Take a gentleman friend with you," she urged. "Take a bodyguard, someone you feel comfortable with."

Official confirmation of the identity of the remains pulled from the forest grave was made later that day when dental records were checked against the teeth of the young woman pulled from the sandy forest grave. They were a perfect match.

EIGHT

More Vanished Girls

Could Charles Rathbun be a serial slayer?

That was the question being posed by Los Angeles County Sheriff Sherman Block, who referred to the suspected murderer of the model as a "possible serial killer." Block said Rathbun was a suspect in the murder of Kimberly Pandelios and added that investigators were told she and the photographer were acquainted with each other.

"We are now including the Pandelios case as a formal part of this investigation," he announced at a news conference.

The sheriff also mentioned, rather ominously, that since Rathbun's arrest, several women had told about brushes with the photographer when he made "overtures for sexual favors . . . sometimes on photo shoots, sometimes in other relationships." Block characterized Rathbun as having been "pushy."

It wasn't the first time women complained of sexually aggressive behavior by the photographer, and the onetime undercover vice cop turned administrator wasn't the first to use the word *pushy* to describe his never-say-die attitude when he was rejected by a desirable woman.

The feisty veteran lawman was outspoken and attracted national publicity a few months earlier when he publicly criticized Superior Court Judge Lance Ito for removing three white deputies from bailiff duty with the O. J. Simpson jury after a single black juror complained they were biased. Block remarked that the bailiffs were following the judge's own orders, which were very specific about how the sequestered jurors were to be treated.

The blunt-speaking sheriff's latest remarks about the new case rattling the Southland plunged him back in the spotlight, and although they would come back to haunt him, nevertheless he had posed a question pondered at least briefly in one way or another by a rapidly burgeoning number of homicide investigators in jurisdictions from suburban Los Angeles to the Midwest.

Widespread publicity over the search for Linda, Rathbun's arrest, and discovery of her body, sparked a flurry of activity across the country as well as in California, by police detectives investigating unsolved murders and mysterious vanishings of attractive young women.

In communities where the gangly photographer with the thinning rust-colored hair was known to have traveled or settled for a time, and in some areas where it was only suspected he may have visited, investigators began taking close new looks at cold cases and dusting off old files to check out the possibilities he might have the answers they were seeking.

They were looking for similarities in such matters as the victim profile and the methods in which the murders were carried out—even such details as how bodies were disposed of. The unsolved cases of missing and murdered models, or especially attractive college coeds and other women and girls who fit or came close to resembling Linda Sobek and Kim Pandelios in physical appearance, interests, and activities, were being given particularly close scrutiny.

The hundreds of telephone calls made to the Los Angeles Sheriff's Department and the HBPD with tips or suspicions from private citizens played a big part in the decision to assemble the task force working on the Sobek case. The group varied in number but at times as many as twenty detectives were assigned to it and several of them were kept busy checking out information and queries from the flood of telephone calls. A Sheriff's Department spokesman pointed out it was better to assign a large team of detectives to check out the leads promptly than to put a couple of people on the case and wait a year for them to plow through the mass of work.

There was nothing unusual about looking for a connection with other possible crimes. It's standard operational procedure when suspects are named or arrested in serial murders or high-profile cases such as the Sobek case. That can be true even when the suspect doesn't show the classic signs that so many serial killers exhibit. There was no indication Rathbun was enjoying his notoriety and looking to carve out a special niche for himself as one of the enduring ogres in modern American criminal history like Manson or serial killers Jeffrey Dahmer and John Wayne Gacy, Jr.

Rathbun didn't leap at the opportunity to impress interrogators with any self-perceived brilliance in getting away with repeated murders by reciting a list of victims, dates, places, and locations. He didn't deliberately court the press. And he didn't form any early relationships with groupies attracted by his sudden dark celebrity. Even so, California police were deeply interested in his central Ohio ties, and within a couple of days of his arrest in Hollywood, a pair of homicide investigators from the Los Angeles County Sheriff's Department walked off a passenger jetliner at the Port Columbus International Airport where they were met by local officers. The visitors were in town to work on their profile of Rathbun's background, on a timeline sequence of his activities, and to look over and discuss carefully selected unsolved homicides in the area.

Sheriff Block had disclosed during one of the news conferences that he was sending detectives ''out of state . . . to look at some unresolved cases in areas where we know Rathbun has been and there are possibilities that he may have been involved in homicide cases in those areas. One in particular that we are looking at is a homicide in Ohio, in close proximity to where Rathbun's father lives and where Rathbun has visited," he declared.

While the LASD homicide detectives were in Columbus they met with the photographer's former girlfriend, Karen Masullo. Details of the conversation, held on Friday morning, December 1, weren't publicly revealed. But Mrs. Masullo disclosed to reporters before the meeting that she planned to tell them about disturbing changes in his personality she noticed a few years earlier. She told the *Dispatch* that initially she was pleased that someone cared enough to pay so much attention to her, but her old friend's continued obsession with her soon became tiring. "My husband loves me," she said, "but Charlie coveted me."

The Los Angeles detectives also talked with Rathbun's relatives in the Columbus area before moving on to Lansing, where they had more conversations with local police and former associates or friends of the murder suspect.

Lansing homicide investigator John Hersman had previously telephoned California and told police probing the Rathbun case that the photographer had local ties. The Michigan detective also advised his West Coast colleagues about the mysterious vanishing of a young Lansing woman who had lived less than one mile from a trailer park Rathbun formerly listed as his address. After filling the California sleuths in on the local probe during the phone call, Hersman put together a package of information collected while investigating the disappearance of Rose Larner, and mailed it to them. The information was ultimately shared with members of the California task force, along with data on other cases of homicides or vanishings of women Rathbun could have possibly been involved with during his cross-country travels.

Another homicide task force composed of investigators from law enforcement agencies in the Lansing area, including Ingham, Eaton, and Clinton counties, took over the Larner probe. Officers from the Michigan State Police Department, East Lansing, and Meridian township were also part of the team effort. Members of the multiagency police team sent photos of Ms. Larner and of two other area women, whose mystifying disappearances were under investigation, to their colleagues in California. The pictures of Ms. Larner, Paige Marie Renkoski, and of Christine O'Brien were to be checked against the photos of women that were seized by investigators from Rathbun's Hollywood apartment.

According to the data rounded up by the veteran Michigan law officers, Rathbun continued to maintain a mailing address at the Stonegate trailer park just south of Lansing in Delhi township into at least 1993, the year his pretty teenage neighbor vanished as suddenly and completely as if she were whisked aboard a passing UFO.

The eighteen-year-old girl, whose friends and family usually called by her nickname, "Rosie," was last seen by her mother, Rose Markey, on December 7, 1993. Before stepping out of a friend's house on Midwood Street on Lansing's south side into the prewinter chill at about 2:30 A.M., the teenager pulled a warm brown coat over her sweater and blue jeans and snuggled a gray and white hat over her shoulder-length brown hair. She was such a confirmed night person that family members affectionately joked about the girl who slept the day away then boogied from sundown to sunup. They called her "the vampire."

Nevertheless, Mrs. Markey didn't like the idea of the pretty, petite, five foot one inch, 110-pound girl walking into the night by herself and urged her to drive the family van. But she was in the mood to walk.

"Rosie, I love you," her mother called. "I love you too," the girl called back. Then the self-confident, chatty teenager walked off into the darkness, planning to hike several blocks to her boyfriend's house on nearby Jolly Road. Mrs. Markey never again saw her daughter, or heard the voice of the talkative girl who was known for spending hours on the telephone and for dreamily discussing plans of some day becoming a police officer like a favorite uncle in Wisconsin—or of going into modeling.

Rosie loved the telephone so much that some of her acquaintances changed the numbers on their pagers to keep her from bothering them. Sometimes she made as many as 1,200 calls in a single month. But the motor-mouthed teenager never called her mother or anyone else after the dark, gloomy night she walked out of the house in Lansing for the last time.

Months later her mother told a reporter that she realized on Christmas Day when her daughter's brightly wrapped presents were left unopened, that she would never again see the brash, hazel-eyed girl. Rosie loved holidays and presents and if she had a choice in the matter she wouldn't have missed sharing the occasion with her mother and other family members.

Police took Rosie's ominous disappearance seriously from the very beginning, and officers carefully retraced the route it was believed she would have taken to her boyfriend's home, meticulously combing the streets, sidewalks, and frozen lawns for clues. Shortly after Rosie vanished, a neighbor who lived only one block from Midland told police she had looked through her window and noticed a young woman walking nearby about the time the irrepressible teenager set out on foot for her boyfriend's house. The neighbor said a car was cruising slowly in the street beside the girl and it seemed someone was trying to coax her into accepting a ride.

During the next two years Lansing police, county sheriff's officers, and investigators from the Michigan State Police Department searched more than fifty different locations looking for Rosie's body.

Investigators believed she was murdered, and they scoured city parks and tramped through dense tracts of woods on private land. Divers from the Michigan State Police Department slowly coasted along the cluttered bottoms of isolated ponds and abandoned gravel pits fruitlessly peering through the murky waters looking for a body.

Police even used specially trained dogs to sniff for the poisonous gasses produced by decaying human bodies, and dug through four-inch concrete under the basement stairway of a big house in East Lansing. The Montie House was a cooperative primarily tenanted by students enrolled at Michigan State University, but after police chopped up the cement floor the lawmen and their canine sniffers found nothing more ominous than another layer of older wooden flooring under the newly created rubble.

Another time a Michigan State Police helicopter skimmed low over the muddy waters of the Grand River after a tipster indicated Rosie's body was dumped there. If the tip was legitimate the body had floated away, was moved by somone, or something else happened to it. The search of the river was as fruitless and disappointing as earlier efforts focused on other locations.

The girl was missing nearly two years when several tips led police to a rugged tract of state-owned property in Northeast Michigan's Gladwin County about eighty-five miles from the capital city. The reports raised a flurry of excitement over the possibility that the puzzle was at long last about to be solved, but investigators once more came up empty-handed.

Police and members of the missing girl's family even talked with psychics, and three of the sensitives, without being advised about the conclusions of their clairvoyant brethren, came up with the same determinations: Rosie's remains were secreted away near a group of earthen mounds in the Lansing area. A scatter of bones was eventually uncovered in the area of the mounds, but after inspection by experts they were quickly ruled out as having nothing to do with the mystery. They were the remains of a dog or some other canine.

Despite the massive police search, law enforcement authorities were unable to turn up any trace of the missing girl. But the case was kept open and every new tip and possibility was faithfully followed up by Detective Hersman and his colleagues.

A task force spokesman indicated they were continuing to take a good look at Rathbun in the Larner case even though other developments appeared to be more promising. The state police sergeant added that the possibility Rathbun had something to do with the disappearance was "remote." Neither family members nor friends of the missing girl were aware of any acquaintance between her and the photographer.

Yet, certain facts couldn't be ignored. Investigators confirmed that Rathbun was in Lansing in June 1993 and during the following spring. He had friends who lived in a mobile home in Delhi township. Rosie was young, pretty, and was toying with the idea of trying to become a professional model. She was exactly the kind of impressionable teenager whose trust conceivably could be won by an experienced photographer with a portfolio full of glamour pictures of lovely models about her age, a thick list of magazine, calendar, and advertising credits, and a glib spiel.

By the time Rathbun came to the attention of Michigan police, local and state homicide investigators were up to their ears in probes of missing or murdered young women. One of the most baffling was tied to a five-year-old mystery surrounding the disappearance of thirty-year-old Paige Renkoski.

Paige was a statuesque five foot seven inch, blue-eyed blonde with a model's figure, who disappeared after stopping her car at the side of busy Interstate 96 near the Fowlerville exit a few miles east of Lansing on May 24, 1990. The substitute schoolteacher's silver 1986

Oldsmobile Cutlass Calais sat undisturbed on the westbound shoulder of the busy highway for five hours before police stopped in the late afternoon to investigate after being alerted by a passing motorist. The driver side door was open, the engine was still running, and the headlights were on. The woman's purse and shoes were inside, and there was no damage to the vehicle or any traces of blood.

Earlier in the day Paige had driven her mother, Ardis Renkoski, to the Detroit Metro-Wayne County Airport, and after stopping to visit a girlfriend, she was returning to her home in the upscale northeast Lansing suburb of Okemos when she vanished. Her car was abandoned along a busy stretch of the interstate between Lansing and Detroit about twenty miles from her exit.

Police quickly broadcast a description of the missing woman detailing her appearance down to her shoulder-length hairstyle and surgical scars on her right arm. She was described as wearing a long-sleeve, white turtleneck shirt, multicolored baggy silk slacks and a green and gold beaded necklace. Five-thousand flyers with her photo and a typewritten description were printed and distributed, and within a few days a twenty-five thousand dollar reward for information leading to her safe return or the arrest and conviction of her abductor was also posted.

Investigators brought in nine tracker dogs to help them comb through a densely wooded area near the highway exit, while a helicopter crisscrossed the skies a few hundred feet overhead without any success.

Among the most promising of hundreds of leads developed by investigators, were reports from several motorists who said they saw the woman standing in front of her car talking to a man with a maroon minivan. The van carried Michigan license plates and was either a Chrysler or a GMC, they said.

Livingston County Sheriff's Detectives and other law enforcement agencies were still hoping to solve the puzzle of the missing teacher when Rathbun was arrested in California and they learned of his local connection. Paige shared many of the same physical characteristics as Linda, including the color of their hair and eyes. The two women were also close to the same age when they vanished.

The third missing Michigan woman whose photo was sent to Los Angeles to be compared with pictures found in the photographer's house was tied to a much more recent disappearance. Twenty-four-year-old Christine O'Brien vanished in Livingston County in circumstances eerily similar to the disappearance of Paige Renkoski.

The five foot one inch, 100-pound woman was last seen early Tuesday evening, July 18, 1995, when she paid a bill at a health spa in the industrial city of Flint a few miles northeast of Lansing. She was an enthusiastic equestrienne and told an employee at the spa that she was in a hurry because she planned to meet someone who was building horse stables.

Christine lived in Fenton with her parents, Dan and Brenda O'Brien, a machine repairman for General Motors Corporation and a homemaker. The small town is only a few minutes drive south of Flint along U.S. Road 23, but Christine never returned home that night. And she never telephoned, although she always made sure to let her parents know if she was going to be late.

The O'Briens began searching for their missing daughter that evening, but no trace of her was turned up until the following morning. Her sister, Laura, found the missing woman's silver 1987 Chevy Nova parked at the Tyrone Hills Golf Club. The public golf course was only a short walk from a horse auction in Fenton, which Christine often visited. The car was properly parked, locked, and the keys and her purse were missing.

Family members posted a five thousand dollar reward for information about the whereabouts of the attractive young woman with the brown eyes and long brown hair; helicopters and tracking dogs were used in two massive searches; and police investigated hundreds of leads without success. Many of the same officers who helped comb area fields and woods for Paige Renkoski also participated in the fruitless search for Christine O'Brien.

Michigan investigators also checked briefly for a possible link between Rathbun and one of the state's most notorious unsolved murders in recent years, the sex slaying of a pretty Northwest Airlines stewardess who was raped, tortured, and butchered minutes after walking into her hotel room at the edge of the Detroit Metro-Wayne County Airport in Romulus.

Forty-one-year-old Nancy Jean Ludwig was a fifteen-year-veteran stewardess, when her plane landed at the airport at 7:51 P.M., on February 17, 1991, at the end of a flight from Las Vegas. A few minutes later she and another stewardess left their shuttle van and checked into the 268-room Hilton Airport Inn which contracted to provide housing for air crews on layovers. The last time her colleague saw her was about 9 P.M. when they parted on the third floor, and Nancy began walking down the hallway toward Room 354 near a stairwell, pulling her luggage cart behind her.

A few minutes before 1 P.M. the next day a housekeeper at last disregarded the DO NOT DISTURB sign hung on the front of the door, slipped a plastic key into the lock, and entered the room. The naked body of the five-foot, 105-pound stewardess from suburban Minneapolis was lying facedown on one of the beds covered with a bedspread. A gag was still in her mouth, her throat was slit, and her head and upper body were drenched with blood. Her hands were scarred with deep slashes either from a very sharp knife or a razor, indicating the terrified woman had thrown them up in a vain effort to defend herself. She had been bound with a rope and raped twice, apparently once on each bed.

The woman's underpants, brassiere, panty hose, uniform, jewelry, billfold, and luggage were missing, and police and experts in abnormal psychology later speculated they were kept by the killer as grisly trophies of his crime.

Despite a massive police search for the killer, the promotional efforts of her husband, Art Ludwig, a recently retired program director and vice president with a Minneapolis television station, and a huge eighty thousand dollar reward the case bogged down. Investigators followed up more than two thousand leads and suspected that the killer of the stewardess was lurking in the stairwell and pounced on her as she opened her door and turned or stooped to pull her luggage inside.

Like their colleagues seeking to clear up unsolved slayings in other jurisdictions, investigators from the Romulus Police Department and the Michigan State Police took a close look at the possibility the photographer might have been involved in the case. But Rathbun was not a good match for the psychological profile of Mrs. Ludwig's killer that was developed by Michigan State Police. According to the profile, the sex slayer was white, in his thirties, probably had been released from a psychiatric hospital shortly before the killing, worked in or near the hotel, and knew beforehand that stewardesses stayed there on their layovers. Rathbun is white and was in his early thirties when the stewardess was slain, but that is about as close as he came to matching the profile.

There were other more solidly scientific reasons to eliminate him as a suspect, as well. The killer left samples of his DNA code behind in the blood splattered hotel room with the mutilated body of his petite victim. The FBI ran a DNA profile on tissue believed to have come from the killer, and subsequently more than two hundred men were eliminated as possible suspects through blood and saliva comparisons.

Early in December after Rathbun's arrest, Romulus police announced that he, too, was eliminated as a suspect in the savage sex slaying of the stewardess. Laboratory analysts compared samples of his blood and DNA with the tissue believed to belong to the killer, and the unique genetic codes did not match.

Even though Rathbun was eliminated as a possible suspect in the Ludwig slaying, he hadn't yet been ruled out as a possible serial killer. Homicide detectives across the country probing other murders were just as devoted as their colleagues in Romulus were to solving their own baffling cases.

In Columbus police were taking a close look at Rathbun and at an accused serial killer arrested after an alleged cross-country murder spree, as possible suspects in the slaying of an Ohio State University coed, eighteen-year-old Stephanie L. Hummer, in 1994.

Coincidentally, hard-drinking drifter and occasional carnival roustabout Glen Rogers was nabbed following a wild high-speed state police chase through the hills of rural Kentucky on November 13, only nine days before Rathbun was picked up as a suspect in the Sobek killing. Rogers was accused of committing a string of homicides including the slaying of a Southern California woman. Like Rathbun, Rogers grew to adulthood in Ohio then trekked west to California.

Both Rathbun and Rogers were men who had uniquely tempting backgrounds, and techniques or abilities that could have potentially been used to attract shapely women. Spur-of-the-moment killers as well as conniving serial slayers who sometimes plan their crimes beforehand in great detail, often use props to lure their victims. Ted Bundy, who was a classic serial killer of young women, typically lulled the natural suspicions of his victims by wearing an arm sling or hobbling about on crutches and asking for help with some light physical task such as loading a surfboard onto the roof of his parked VW Bug.

Rogers allegedly depended on nothing more than his rugged good looks and a rough-hewn, backwoods charm to lure sexy females into his clutches. He didn't bother with inanimate props. But Rathbun had his camera and an impressive portfolio as possible bait, if he chose to use them for sinister purposes. The prospect of sudden riches and fame could be a powerful lure for naively trusting young women with visions of being "discovered" by a big-time photographer and launching exciting careers in modeling. Rathbun, of course, was a frequent visitor to Columbus and to Worthington, and he returned to his old stomping grounds at least four or five times a year.

The victim of the baffling murder that had puzzled homicide investigators in Columbus for nearly two years, was young and had the fresh-faced beauty and sleek, firm body that could have qualified her for the fling at modeling, which she is said to have had aspirations of undertaking. Detectives, however, were apparently unable to locate anyone who could place Rathbun and the pretty college girl together or confirm that they were acquaintances.

A freshman honors student from Cincinnati, Stephanie was selected as an Evans Scholar, one of the young women and men who have worked as golf caddies and are helped with college tuition as part of a program to help promote and support their higher education. Scholars are nominated by their country clubs during the junior year of high school and must graduate in the top 20 percent of their classes to qualify.

The scholarship winner was enjoying an informal reunion on campus with former high school friends, when she was abducted between 3:30 and 4:30 Sunday morning, March 6. Early Saturday, Stephanie's parents, both OSU graduates, visited and treated her and her chums to lunch. Later, after Daniel and Susan Hummer left, the young people watched movies and played cards throughout Saturday evening and into the wee hours of the next morning before leaving Stephanie's residence at the Evans Scholars House on their way to a party over a campus bar.

One of the boys in the group slashed his hand trying

to vault a chain-link fence and he and his male roommate left to run cold water over the cut. Amie Nelson, a Northwestern University student and the other member of the quartet, decided she wanted to return to the Evans Scholars House and left after Stephanie gave her room key to her. Investigators later surmised that Stephanie was abducted while she was cutting through Pearl Alley, a well-lighted route just east of the campus and about a block from the Evans Scholars House.

About nine or ten hours later her body was found lying facedown in an isolated brush filled field west of the main business area of the city, two and a half miles from the alley. Authorities were tipped off after the corpse was spotted by a sharp-eyed crewman on a passing Conrail freight train. The body was naked except for a bra, tennis shoes, and socks. The rest of her clothes, including a blue nylon windbreaker with a hood and a front logo printed in green letters, "Evans Scholars, Winter Formal 1994," black denim slacks, a blue denim shirt, and a black body suit, were missing.

Detectives theorized she was abducted by a stranger and stripped before being forced to walk from a car through a heavy stand of brambles to a clearing near the railroad tracks a short distance from the Scioto River. She was smashed on the back of the head with a heavy object and strangled at the same location where the body was found. The girl from Cincinnati, who only a few months before urged her high school classmates to blaze new paths in their lives and "leave a trail," was the victim of an incredibly brutal murder. The ambitiously optimistic advice from the girl whose teachers described as an overachiever was printed in the 1993 high school yearbook. Stephanie was the editor.

Although the autopsy indicated she was involved in sexual activity shortly before her slaying, questions developed over whether or not she was raped. Dr. Cyril Wecht, a former coroner and one of the most famous forensic pathologists in the nation, advised that the au-

topsy didn't support a conclusion of rape. There were
no signs of struggle and no traces of blood or other
foreign tissue under her fingernails indicating she
scratched or hit at an assailant, according to the autopsy
report.

After Sheriff Block announced that authorities in Ohio
were interested in the photographer as a possible suspect
in a murder there, Columbus, police responded cau-
tiously to the disclosure. They played it close to the vest
with the local press, but the city's media quickly revealed investigators were checking out Rathbun to determine if he could have been involved in the unsolved
Hummer slaying. Homicide Detective Pat Barr refused
to definitely identify Rathbun as a suspect but indicated
he was one of various people who were being looked at
in the case. Since the coed's murder, Columbus police
had already checked out more than sixty suspects.

The key to the possibility of Rathbun's involvement
was linked to whether or not he was in Columbus on
the weekend of the slaying. The same weekend Stephanie was killed, a bodybuilding competition for men
and women called the Arnold Schwarzenegger Classic,
was being held in the city. Rathbun was known to be
fond of photographing male and female bodybuilders
during workouts, but a records check failed to disclose
his name among reporters or photographers with media
credentials for the show named after the famous body-
builder and Hollywood film hero.

The bodybuilding event at the Veterans' Memorial
was staged only one week after the Columbus International Auto Show, a production that would also have
been of considerable interest to the gallivanting photographer. The auto show is one of the largest such events
in the nation and provides an extraordinarily attractive
showcase where professionals from every area of the
industry can view the latest advances in automotive design and technology. For a highly skilled automotive
photographer such as Rathbun, the event could also offer

an excellent opportunity to strengthen and renew personal contacts with professionals in the fields of promotion, advertising, and publishing. It was an event he could have been expected to do his best to attend.

Early in December, however, Columbus police announced their determination: Rathbun was not involved in the murder of the local coed. Furthermore, Police Lieutenant Dan Wood told reporters authorities did not believe he was involved in any other unsolved slayings in the area.

But police in the nearby central Ohio city of Lancaster also briefly looked into the possibility that a solution to the community's most baffling and longest unsolved murder might somehow have a connection to the former Columbus resident who was charged with a grisly slaying halfway across the country. The victim in Lancaster was a high school student with the same kind of youthful beauty and zestful appearance that fit in with the faces and figures of teenage models appearing on covers of major national magazines aimed at young girls like *Seventeen* and *Teen Beat*.

The case files on the shocking murder of seventeen-year-old Stacey Fairchild almost seven years earlier were yellowing with age, but there was no crime in the history of the quiet community of about thirty-five thousand people, thirty-eight miles southeast of Columbus, that homicide investigators were more determined to solve.

The high school girl had a part-time job at the Fairfield Mall. On the night of February 2, 1989, she left work, climbed into her car, and drove into eternity. She never reached her home. A massive search for the missing teenager didn't end until three days later when her body was discovered caught in a tangle of branches and driftwood in the icy Hocking River that runs through Fairfield County, the core of the city, and behind the mall. Her burned-out car was found a few miles upstream. An autopsy disclosed that although she was beaten on the back of the head, her death was caused by drowning. The brutal murder sent shockwaves through the placid community, where people were used to leaving the keys in their cars and often didn't bother to lock their doors at night. The slaying of an innocent high school girl was the kind of crime that more often occurred in larger, more rowdy communities like Columbus, Cleveland, or Cincinnati. It was definitely not typical of a friendly town like Lancaster.

For a long time after the teenager's pitiful frozen corpse was pulled from the river, grown women and girls didn't move around outside their homes at night unless they were accompanied by an adult male companion—often armed with a gun. People also began locking their doors at night and taking their keys with them when they left their cars. The fright eventually died down, but despite the best efforts of homicide detectives, who interviewed scores of people and followed up hundreds of leads, the puzzle over the identity of the mysterious killer was never solved. Like others before him, Rathbun was also ultimately eliminated as a possible suspect in the Fairchild murder.

News of the developments in the Midwest, where police in two states indicated they were no longer looking at Rathbun as a serious suspect in unsolved slayings or disappearances, drew sharp criticism of the Los Angeles County Sheriff from the photographer's legal counsel. The sheriff was accused of behaving irresponsibly by labeling the photographer as a possible serial killer before developing any evidence to support the accusations.

At this writing, Rathbun had not been linked or charged in any murders or disappearances outside California. In California, while Rathbun has not been officially eliminated as one of the possible suspects in the Pandelios case—which remains open and unsolved—authorities have said that they do not have any evidence that would warrant bringing any charges against him. The only charges pending against Rathbun, as of this writing, are in connection with the Sobek case.

NINE

A Murder Charge

The nagging pain of not knowing was over for Linda Sobek's family and for her friends. But the sense of relief was bittersweet; a mixed blessing.

At the house in Hermosa Beach wreaths, bouquets, and plants with large chunks of stone spotted conspicuously among some of the flowers were placed at the front entrance and on porches. The stones were brightly painted, and messages of love and hope were scrawled on the rough surfaces. "Surf's Up," said one.

At the Sobek home in Lakewood, as it had for several days, a yellow ribbon hung over the address number. A photo of Linda was propped up on the porch just outside the front door where it was surrounded by poinsettias, arrangements of cut flowers, and lighted or half-melted candles. Inside, the Sobek home was filled with family, neighbors, and with Raiderettes, models, their boyfriends, and others who flocked there to comfort the parents and share their grief. Fat bundles of letters and cards, most of them from strangers, were delivered daily to the house with messages of sympathy and support.

Robert Sobek told reporters he would love to have his daughter still at home, but he was relieved that the waiting was ended. "I think she's in heaven, I think this was her time, as it will be when our time comes," he told a newspaper reporter.

On the Sunday morning following recovery of the model's remains, about fifty of her friends and family members, including many who arrived from out of town or out of state, gathered at the Baycities Community Church in Redondo Beach to pray for her. Throughout the ordeal, Linda's family had found comfort in their spirituality and firm religious belief.

A cousin who drove downstate from San Jose with his wife and two teenage daughters, described Linda to reporters as "one of the diamonds of our family . . ."

The next day, family members drove to the site of Linda's makeshift grave in the forest wash and placed flowers there. But the real closure wouldn't occur until she was properly mourned and reburied. And that couldn't take place until pathologists at the Los Angeles County Department of Chief Medical Examiner-Coroner had completed an autopsy. The tongue-twisting name for the facility adjacent to the Los Angeles County-USC Medical Center is typical bureaucrateze for the county coroner's office and morgue.

The coroner's office, like the Los Angeles Police Department, had been the subject of intense criticism and bad press for years. The most recent peak of criticism directed at the department occurred during the Simpson trial when a medical examiner was tied to embarrassing missteps while conducting autopsies on the victims. Although not rivaling the recent carnival at the downtown Los Angeles Criminal Courts Building on West Temple Street for media hysteria, the search for the missing model attracted international attention. No one in the law enforcement community, including the coroner, wanted to do anything that would open the door to a new wave of public criticism.

Linda's autopsy was conducted in the antiseptic environment of the Coroner's Office with extreme care and professionalism. Her cadaver was loaded onto a gurney and wheeled onto a large scale where it was weighed; her height was measured; the tips of her fingers and

thumbs were inked and the images impressed on finger-
print cards; and full body X rays were taken. Just like
the depictions in movies of bodies in morgues, an identification tag was already looped around one of her big
toes. Then the body she had shaped, molded, and protected with such fidelity and passionate attention was
wheeled into one of two autopsy rooms at the morgue
and laid out on a flat metal table equipped with drains
at the sides for runoff fluids. The table had been used
before for hundreds of other autopsies.

On dissecting tables, corpses take on a distressing
similarity. Female or male, white or black, rich or poor,
short and fat, or tall and skinny, they're all very much
the same; lumps of cold, pasty flesh, the mute repository
of secrets to be unlocked by the scalpel and the microscope.

In the same room a few feet away from the table on
which Linda's body was stretched, other autopsy teams
were already at work creating a curious buzz of life
while surrounded by death. The pathologists seemed
oblivious to the new arrival while they expertly plumbed
the gelid matter, seeking to unravel death's most intimate and closely guarded mysteries. The busy room was
a bewilderment of body trays, stainless steel pans, hanging scales for weighing organs, corrosive odors, floor
mops, and metal buckets.

Considering the length of time Linda's body had lain
eighteen inches under the thin covering of dirt and stone
during the hot, dry days, and the moist, cool evenings
when heavy mists of fog as thick as cream hugged the
ravines and mountaintops, it was in remarkably good
condition. Surprisingly little decomposition had occurred, and some of the medical professionals theorized
it was because of the chill nights. Her body was found
downmountain, and valleys are colder than hillsides.

Pathologists wearing masks over faces and noses, la-
tex gloves, plastic aprons, and shoe covers, had bent
over the same shiny silvery slab on which Linda was

laid out to slice and probe at the corpses of people who were shot, stabbed, slashed with machetes, beaten, and tossed off buildings. Men and women wound up on the table after dying of drug overdoses, in gang shootings, fires, drownings, and being brutally mangled in grinding traffic accidents on the maze of streets and expressways that stretch in and around Los Angeles.

There are myriad ways to die violently in Los Angeles County. And anyone who dies by violence, or in suspicious circumstances is a candidate for the autopsy table.

Most of the victims of ''Nightstalker'' Richard Ramirez, a coke-snorting self-described Satanist who prowled the Los Angeles suburbs on a two-year rampage of robbery, rape, and murder were autopsied at the busy morgue. More recently, the bodies of twin-murder victims Nicole Brown Simpson and Ronald Lyle Goldman were wheeled into the autopsy room on gurneys after being butchered just outside Mrs. Simpson's toney town house in Brentwood.

Every year in Los Angeles County, the coroner investigates about nineteen thousand deaths, and approximately seven thousand autopsies are conducted on men, women, and children. About one in every four persons who dies in Los Angeles winds up at the morgue. It is the second busiest medical examiner's office in the country, trailing only behind New York City.

The crushing workload is one of the main reasons the department has been plagued with problems and criticism. There are simply too many bodies, and not enough pathologists and support staff. For awhile a few years earlier, cadavers were stacked up for four or five days before overworked pathologists could get to them. When employees walked into the huge refrigerator where the bodies were stored, they wore gas masks because of the awful odor of formaldehyde and decomposing flesh.

Long before Linda's body was wheeled into the antiseptic morgue in downtown Los Angeles, those problems had eased. But the new coroner, Dr. Lakshamanan Sathyavagiswaran, and his industrious staff of seventeen pathologists, still had all they could do to keep pace with the backbreaking workload.

Senior Deputy Medical Examiner, Dr. James K. Ribe, one of the coroner's leading pathologists, was assigned to conduct the autopsy on the pretty model. Representatives from the Sheriff's Department and the Hermosa Beach Police Department witnessed the autopsy, unobtrusively watching every step of the process.

Linda's body was given swift and painstaking attention. As every homicide detective knows, the early hours of an investigation are crucial. The memories of witnesses, as well as the value of physical evidence overlooked for too long, can quickly fade and blur. If too much time was allowed to lapse before precise determinations were made about the exact cause of death and other factors tied to the autopsy process were pinned down, the investigation of the suspicious death could be seriously slowed. Results of important tests on blood and tissue samples can also be altered if a cadaver has gone unexamined for too long. The body the pathologists were preparing to autopsy had already been prey to insects and weather in its lonely makeshift grave for more than a week.

Before pathologists touched the body with a scalpel, color pictures were taken by an experienced forensic photographer. Those photographs and others taken later in the autopsy process were the last ever snapped of the model.

The next step in the grim process was a close visual study of the cadaver, head to toe, front to back, while it lay on the table fully clothed just as it was unearthed from the grave. After the clothing was removed another visual inspection was made and more pictures were shot, including close-ups of areas that showed signs of injury.

There were no obvious breaks in major bones or knee-level damage, the types of injury that could be expected to occur when someone is suddenly slammed with two tons of furiously spinning metal, glass, and rubber. Numerous bruises were visible on the body, including a large area on one of Linda's cheeks, but it was difficult to immediately determine the cause. There were various eventualities, including the possibility they were caused by injuries from the accident described by Rathbun, by an unrelated mishap prior to death, trauma during or after burial in the makeshift grave, or by coagulating blood. That was something to be determined with more certainty after laboratory analysis.

Scrapings were also gathered from under Linda's fingernails. Laboratory tests would be conducted later on the nail scrapings to determine if they matched the suspect's blood type. If a match turned up, it could be an indication that a struggle occurred before her death.

At last, the dissection began and the pathologist began probing at the spongy flesh with his fingers and a scalpel. He examined the fragile bones in the neck and deftly sliced through the skin, the thin layer of fat, and the firm, smooth muscle the girl had worked so assiduously to develop and shape. Samples of blood, urine, brain matter, and other body tissue were collected to be analyzed later by serologists and other laboratory technicians. Scans would reveal the possible presence of any alcohol, prescription and over-the-counter drugs, or illicit substances.

Pathologists share a unique and grisly physical intimacy with their subjects while they examine and take samples of internal organs and other matter. When their work was completed, the coldly efficient forensic pathologists would know more about how the body of the health and exercise enthusiast functioned than she had known herself. Most importantly, presumably they would also know the exact cause of death. They might not be able to learn all the details surrounding the events leading up to her death, but they would know what injuries were fatal—why her heart stopped pumping blood and why her system shut down.

Forensic pathologists can determine what was eaten at the last meal, how far along the digestive process has progressed, and, if the body is that of a woman—sometimes men, as well—if they were involved in recent sexual activity.

When the preliminary autopsy was completed, the conclusions confirmed suspicions of task force investigators that the photographer hadn't told the whole truth about how the model died.

"The findings are not consistent with death due to automobile trauma," Scott Carrier, a spokesman for the Coroner's Department announced to the press. "If you are struck by a vehicle, your legs might be broken. Her legs weren't broken."

There was no sign in the preliminary findings of any injuries that would indicate Linda was either shot, stabbed, or sustained massive head injuries. At that early stage, the coroner wasn't even ruling out the possibility of a drug overdose or poisoning. No immediately visible signs of sexual assault were observed, but more sophisticated tests were still to be conducted. Even then there was the possibility that a conclusive determination might not be possible, because under most circumstances the signs of rape disappear after about twenty-four hours.

For the time being, however, authorities weren't yet ready to say just exactly how they believed the young woman was killed. Carrier said that wouldn't be determined until the results of various tests were learned, and the process could take several weeks. The coroner was playing it safe, and released information to the clamor of reporters, a bit at a time, only after pathologists were certain of their facts. Homicide investigators were more outspoken. Sheriff's Captain Dan Burt told the press that authorities were "very skeptical" about Rathbun's story.

While tests were still being conducted on the samples taken during the autopsy and the final report apparently was weeks away, Linda's body was at last released to her family and transported to the Luyben Family Mortuary in Long Beach.

In the meantime, stories were already circulating and leaking to the press that the model died of asphyxiation. Willette was the source of one of the reports when he told journalists he heard indirectly from sheriff's officers that Linda was asphyxiated, although he didn't know the details. When they were approached by reporters, law enforcement authorities refused to either confirm or deny the lawyer's statement. A coroner's office spokesman branded the report as "premature."

Premature or not, it was impossible to turn off the waves of speculation and fanciful stories that rolled through the media and circulated among the general public about the report and the autopsy findings. Stories made the rounds that Linda's hands were tied, or she was trussed up hand and foot; she was burned with cigarettes; and that she may have been buried alive.

If the rumors of Linda's asphyxiation were true, her family's hopes that her death was relatively painless, would be irretrievably shredded. It was impossible to hold on any longer to hopes of a quick, relatively painless death for the vibrant beach sprite who had so enriched their lives. Some of Linda's model girlfriends were already confiding to the Sobek family lawyer that they had endured unpleasant experiences with Rathbun and were afraid of him.

The family and Linda's chums decided that the reward, which had grown to one hundred thousand dollars in cash and pledges, would be turned into a memorial fund to help battered women so that her death could bring about positive change. The model's friends were determined that her name and memory would live on, and they organized a fund-raiser named the Linda Sobek Memorial Benefit. Then they donated the twelve hundred dollars that was raised to a battered woman's program headquartered in Redondo Beach. Named 1736

House, the program already operated five shelters for battered women and their children, and executives were planning to open another one soon. The professional football team Linda performed for as a cheerleader, also established a fund in her memory. A spokesman for the Oakland Raiders, which had left Los Angeles and moved upstate to its former home in the Bay Area, announced that the team's Linda Sobek Memorial Fund would also be used to help battered women.

Exactly two weeks after Linda vanished, singly, in pairs, and in small groups, mourners trickled into the funeral home in Long Beach for the visitation. Some of the approximately two hundred people who came to mourn on the first day had never even met the model, but for various reasons they felt especially saddened by the tragedy and throughout the afternoon they seated themselves in the funeral home to quietly share in the final farewell.

Family members, relatives, and close friends bid a more private good-bye at a viewing on Wednesday that was held outside the glare of the media. Linda's heavy oak casket was placed at the front of the chapel surrounded by brilliant splashes of pink carnations, red roses, and a rainbow profusion of other flowers. An easel was set up in front of another abundance of flowers, and displayed a series of black-and-white photographs of the model. An American flag was draped at one side of the display. Synthesizer music played softly in the background while Linda's father knelt at the casket and clasped his hands in silent prayer.

Mourners showed up at Linda's viewings who knew her as a child, who recognized her as a customer in local shops where they worked, and from the post office. Some teenage girls with hopes of beginning one day soon to carve out their own modeling careers also trooped into the mortuary to pay their respects. Tanya Brown, one of Nicole Brown Simpson's sisters, was among the mourners. She was in tears when she told reporters that she felt like she knew Linda and the model made her think of her sister. "It reminded me a lot of Nicole," Tanya told a reporter for the *Breeze*. "It brought me back to a year ago. I felt compelled to be here."

More than twelve hundred people showed up early Friday afternoon, December 1, when Linda's family and friends at last trooped into the Baptist Church of Lakewood on Arbor Road in Long Beach for the closed-casket memorial service. Mourners included current and former Raiderettes and other members of the Raider organization gathered at the church to share in the farewell. Several active and former football players attended, including onetime star running backs Eric Dickerson and Christian Okoye. Dickerson, who was a former All-Pro, told reporters he met Linda at a party four years earlier, and he remembered her sunny smile. She was always cheerful, and always called him "Crazy Eric," he said.

Outside the church, uniformed police officers directed traffic, and although press coverage was heavy it was surprisingly unobtrusive. Many of the reporters, photographers, and others from the electronic media camped along sidewalks across the street from the church to film and record the proceedings.

As Mrs. Sobek walked into the church she told waiting journalists: "Everything is okay. Don't worry. She is in heaven." Inside she took a place in the front row with her husband, their son, and Steve's wife. The five rows immediately behind them were filled with relatives. While mourners were being ushered to seats inside the flower filled church, a violinist and a guitarist played poignant melodies including "Yesterday" and "Over the Rainbow." During the service itself, the song "Linda" was sung a cappella by Georgina Conception, and "Friends" was sung by a duo composed of Charles Inez, a close chum from her childhood, and by Sandy Makinga, wife of the pastor. Finally, with tears streaming down her cheeks, soloist E. J. Sayles sang "Wind Beneath My Wings."

In a printed memorium distributed to mourners special mention was made of the young woman's devotion to her family. The memorium read in part: "Linda, as we know, was a wonderful young woman with a sparkle in her eye and a capability to give her love to others that many can only dream about giving. Her life taught us how to actively reveal our love; how to be a great friend, the importance of family, and especially 'calling your mom every day.'"

Several of Linda's friends from her childhood and from her dual career as a Raiderette and model walked to the front of the church to offer tearful eulogies, recounting especially fond memories. One friend told about the time in junior high school when Linda asked to try on her cheerleading uniform, then set her sights on becoming a cheerleader herself. A Raiderette talked about how Linda was always able to suit up and get ready for a game before the other girls because she had such natural beauty she didn't use much makeup. Six adolescent girls described Linda as a beautiful role model and inspiration whom they looked up to. Several people reminded the mourners of Linda's July baptism and acceptance of Jesus Christ as her Lord and Saviour.

The Reverend Jim Mackinga, pastor of the Baycities church in Redondo Beach, who baptized and led Linda through her spiritual rebirth, officiated at the solemn 2 P.M. funeral. After advising the mourners to honor Linda's life by loving one another as she loved them, and to begin living their lives again, the clergyman added a strong word of caution to her model friends. "Don't work alone," he urged. "Use the buddy system."

Mackinga reminded mourners during his sermon that Linda was much more than a physically beautiful woman. "We remember Linda not in death, in the way she died, but in life through her love for others and her faith," the clergyman said. He posed three questions, then provided the answers for the mourners.

"Where is she now?" he asked. "In heaven, a place so wonderful it cannot be explained or described. How would God want her family and friends to respond today? Go home and in her honor, move on with their lives," he said. "What would she want her loved ones to do? Take care of themselves, love others, and find faith in Christ."

At the conclusion of the moving service, Linda's parents followed along as the polished oak casket, still covered with sprays of flowers, was removed from the church and loaded into a white hearse. While the hearse pulled away, two hundred white doves were released from in front of the church steps as a tribute to the woman who touched the lives of so many in such a loving way. The next day, family members and a handful of Linda's closest friends gathered for a private funeral service.

While the dead model's survivors were dealing with their grief, the wheels of justice were cranking up. Rathbun was charged with first-degree murder and appeared for arraignment in the South Bay Municipal Court in Torrance on the Monday afternoon following his arrest. It was a typical foggy autumn day in the South Bay.

Many of the reporters who flocked to the courthouse had rubbed their journalistic shoulders only a few weeks earlier while covering the marathon Simpson trial, and now they were back in another courtroom to record proceedings in the latest media event. Most were looking for angles and headlines, but a few elitists were grumbling about the public clamor for sensationalism and relative disinterest in events they believed were of more local or national import.

Shackled with handcuffs and a belly chain, dressed in a baggy pale yellow jail jumpsuit, showing a scraggly growth of fresh whiskers, and with both wrists still covered on the inside with adhesive bandages after the razor slashing, Rathbun looked bedraggled and his face was expressionless when he was led before Judge Benjamin Aranda. Heavy black stenciling on the left breast of his uniform identified the prisoner as being confined to the Los Angeles County Jail Hospital.

After leading police to the body, Rathbun was locked in the Men's Central Jail, the same coldly squalid, mouse-colored detention center in downtown Los Angeles where O. J. Simpson was held before and during his twin-murder trial. Like the former football hero, Rathbun was also destined to be held for awhile in the jail's medical unit, which was equipped to observe and protect prisoners with special security needs such as celebrities or those considered to be suicide risks. He was placed under a close suicide watch there. Among other precautions tied to his unique status, he wore a red wristband that identified him as a special care inmate at the detention center, and guards made a visual check on him at least every four hours to ensure that he was unharmed.

Rathbun was isolated from most of the other approximately sixty-two hundred inmates held at the massive concrete and steel fortress, and assigned as the lone occupant of one of the cells. Except for periods when he was meeting with lawyers, scheduled for court appearances, or taking occasional showers he spent almost every hour of every day in the spartanly furnished nine-foot-deep-by-seven-foot-wide concrete cubicle. The cell was equipped with a metal bunk, a stainless steel sink, and a toilet without a lid. A six-inch-by-six-inch window was cut into the barred door.

It was a mind-numbing existence of hours spent alone with little to do except reflect on his personal problems. Reading material was severely restricted, there was no television set in his cell, and meals were solidly institutional and predictably uninspiring. Breakfasts routinely featured scrambled eggs with potatoes or grits along with strong hot coffee. Sometimes the menu was changed to oatmeal or pancakes with an occasional bit of fruit. Lunches were commonly comprised of sandwiches and Kool-Aid. Dinner was a time for hot meals, which could be anything from fried chicken to spaghetti or a hamburger on a bun. During Rathbun's early tenure at the lockup, his meals were delivered to him on a heated kitchen cart and handed through the slot in his steel cell door. The single utensil he was allowed to use for his meals was a plastic spoon. Jailers made sure it was returned with the tray and any leftovers when the prisoner was finished with his meal.

The detention center, like other jails located around the huge county, was jammed to capacity with inmates arrested on charges ranging from forcible rape, drug dealing, and armed robbery to multiple murder. Most of the inmates, usually in the high sixty percentile, were awaiting trials and the others were serving sentences.

A couple of months before Rathbun was locked up at the detention center the population of high-security inmates soared to nearly double the previous number. California's stern new habitual offender law stipulates that anyone convicted of three felonies be sentenced to mandatory terms of from twenty-five years to life in prison. The statute, popularly known as the "three-strikes law," also eliminated probation for anyone convicted of a single felony and precipitously hiked the time that must be served in prison for one- and two-time offenders.

The 1994 law had a lot to do with filling up the jail with inmates awaiting trial for the most serious crimes, because the new rules virtually eliminated prior options to plea bargain for probation or other lesser sentences. If a defendant was a potential three-striker, he or she preferred to take their chances with a judge and jury. The detention center was always a nasty place to be and was populated with ruthless men, many of them members of vicious gangs, who were quick to prey on anyone who showed the slightest sign of weakness. Vulnerable inmates could become victims of everything from threats and extortion to savage beatings and gang rape. When Rathbun was processed into the population, the Men's Central Jail was as dangerous as it had ever been.

Sheriff Block and his corrections team weren't the only authorities with serious problems, however. Everything in Los Angeles County's criminal justice system was on overload. So many felony cases were backed up that the judges and support staff in about fifty civil courts were diverted to handling criminal procedures. In Torrance where Rathbun began his trek through the criminal court system, and in some other Los Angeles County communities, civil trials were completely eliminated for awhile. The new three-strikes law, budget cutbacks, hiring freezes, and plummeting morale all contributed to the troubles. A staggering seventy thousand felony cases annually were being prosecuted in the county, and jails, including the detention center, were filled to capacity with eighteen thousand inmates—the maximum number allowed under a cap ordered by the federal courts.

In the courtroom in Torrance, Judge Aranda peered down from the bench and asked the murder suspect if he understood the proceedings and realized he was waiving his right to a preliminary hearing within ten days of his arraignment. Rathbun blinked his eyes behind his plain round, rimless glasses and softly replied, "I understand." When he was directed to enter a plea, the defendant pleaded not guilty. His voice and demeanor were as lifeless as a zombie.

Rathbun was flanked during the hearing by his newly acquired criminal defense attorney, Mark J. Werksman. The thirty-six-year-old lawyer was a former deputy DA and assistant U.S. attorney with high-rise offices on West Fifth Street in downtown Los Angeles. He had worked on both sides of the fence and paid his dues in the unforgiving crucible of the local and federal courtrooms in Los Angeles. A New York native who was an undergraduate at Yale University and obtained his law degree from the University of Southern California, Werksman was a tough, experienced trial lawyer.

He and his client had the appearance of an incongruous "Mutt and Jeff" duo when they settled themselves at the defense table. Werksman was short, with wavy dark hair, immaculately dressed in a snappy dark suit, and had the look of a man who had just come from a manicure and a fresh hair trim. He was organized and diligently animated. His lanky slump-shouldered client, who towered over him, had thinning rust-colored straight hair, was quiet, subdued, and looked jailhouse miserable in his manacles and rumpled institution suit.

The state was represented at the hearing by Deputy District Attorney Stephen P. Kay. The prosecutor was a twenty-eight-year veteran with the Los Angeles County DA's Office and was best known for his role in the prosecution of some of California's most infamous criminals, Charles Manson and members of his bloodthirsty hippie clan. Kay joined Vincent Bugliosi and a support staff to guide the grueling trials in 1970 and 1971 that finally led to a death sentence for the hypnotic hippie cult leader and for some of his puppetlike followers. Their sentences were commuted to life in prison, with the possibility of parole, after a 1978 U.S. Supreme Court ruling temporarily wiped out death penalty statutes in all of the states.

In early remarks to the press, the bespectacled Deputy DA said he hadn't yet made a decision about seeking the death penalty against Rathbun, although as the charge of murder currently stood it did not qualify for a sentence of capital punishment. But it didn't go unnoticed by the press that even considering Kay's long layoff from frontline courtroom action, he had more death penalty convictions under his belt than any other prosecutor in the county.

Manson was the most infamous of those, but serial killer Lawrence Sigmund Bittaker runs a close second. And some of the similarities between the circumstances surrounding Linda's death and the murder orgy a decade and a half earlier, are eerily striking.

Bittaker teamed up with Roy Lewis Norris, a rapist he served time with at the California Men's Colony in San Luis Obispo, and hatched a scheme to kidnap, rape, torture, and kill teenage girls. Bittaker was released first and bought a van which he nicknamed "Murder Mack." He was soon joined by his pal and for almost a year they terrorized South Bay communities, targeting victims in Redondo Beach and nearby oceanside towns. Their victims ranged in age from thirteen years to nineteen years and they audiotaped their agonized screams and pleas for mercy. They were captured late in 1979 when a woman they abducted in Hermosa Beach broke away after she was raped in the silver van. Norris quickly turned on his pal and told investigators how they approached teenagers on the street to lure them into the murder van with promises of marijuana—or jobs as models.

Each of the men was ultimately charged with five counts of murder, although police recovered hundreds of photographs of young girls during their investigation. Authorities were unable to trace most of them, and the sheriff at that time said he believed the killing pair was linked to another thirty to forty slayings. Some of the bodies and skeletonized remains were recovered from the heavily forested San Gabriel Mountains and San Dimas Canyon, including one with an ice pick still sticking in the skull. Norris eventually pleaded guilty to five counts of murder, turned state's evidence against his confederate, and was sentenced to a prison term of from twenty-five years to life.

In closing arguments at the trial Kay broke into tears while playing a recording the killers made of the agonized shrieks of one of the teenage victims during a torture session. He later remarked that the Manson crimes "pale in comparison" to the Bittaker case. Bittaker is still on death row in San Quentin, the notorious old stone and steel prison in Marin County a few miles north of San Francisco, awaiting the outcome of interminable appeals.

Kay moved away from actively prosecuting murder cases soon after the Bittaker trial in 1981. The last case he personally prosecuted occurred the same year, when he won a burglary conviction without calling the victim as a witness. It was a courtroom feat many of his colleagues doubted could be carried off. By the time he set his sights on the Rathbun case he was leading Deputy DA at the Torrance office.

For roughly fifteen years while Kay concentrated on administrative and supervisory duties with the DA's Office, however, he faithfully attended parole hearings for Bittaker, Manson, and former members of the cult leaders hippie "Family" of killers to argue against their release from prison. He was the first prosecutor ever to go to a state prison to attend parole hearings and boasts that his testimony has helped him compile a perfect 48-and-0 record for his efforts to keep Manson and his followers behind bars.

The fifty-two-year-old career prosecutor decided to personally handle the Rathbun case after working on the probe with Hermosa Beach police and the Sheriff's Department over the long Thanksgiving weekend. He pointed out at a press conference that taking on the task was his idea, not the result of orders from anyone in the main downtown office. The father of three noted that he had two daughters and closely identified with the Sobeks. "My heart goes out to them," he said of Linda's family. He added that several elements in the case reminded him of Bittaker. "The mountain search for a body . . . a nice young woman."

Kay's decision to return to the courtroom was popular with other professionals in the criminal justice business, including prosecutors and police, as well as with the local news media. His mother was a journalist, and he has a history of good relations with the press. Some admirers, pointing to his unobtrusively neat appearance, slender build, dark hair, plain glasses, reputation as a straight shooter, and courtroom heroics have privately and affectionately referred to him as "Clark Kent."

The veteran prosecutor handpicked an experienced colleague, Deputy DA Mary Jean Bowman, as his co-counsel for the Rathbun proceeding. Fiercely capable attorneys were lined up on both sides, and the stage was set for a hard fought case.

It was fairly obvious that Rathbun was going to remain at the detention center for at least several months, and possibly much longer. Werksman was concerned with the photographer's physical comforts and welfare, and during the court appearance asked the judge to issue an order permitting Rathbun to shave and to make telephone calls to his lawyer and to family members.

"Well, we have a little problem with shaving because he tried to commit suicide with a razor," Kay pointed out.

Despite the mild objection, Judge Aranda agreed to most of Werksman's requests, including a proposal to set a hearing to consider a reduction in bail for the defendant. In the meantime bail was continued at one million dollars, and the judge concluded the brief proceeding by designating January 5, 1996, for scheduling of a preliminary hearing.

Preliminary hearings are generally considered to be the most important of all the pretrial proceedings. It is at the conclusion of the hearings that the judge decides if indeed a crime has been committed, and if so, if there is reasonable and probable cause to believe the defendant was the person who did it. If the judge is convinced that the answer to both questions is yes, the defendant is ordered to stand trial.

In one sense, preliminary hearings are minitrials when prosecutors reveal much of their evidence, who their witnesses are going to be, and outline the reasons they think the defendant should be put on trial. The defense gets its first crack at witnesses during the hearings, and usually by the conclusion, observers have gotten a good look at the general strategy planned by both sides for the trial itself. But there was still considerable planning, tactical maneuvering, and tense courtroom skirmishes to be worked through while both sides in the Rathbun case angled for leverage and advantages in the few weeks remaining before the big rehearsal for the main event.

Replying to questions by reporters outside the courtroom who asked about the wisdom of permitting Rathbun to have a razor, Werksman said he didn't believe his client was suicidal any longer. Rathbun was continuing to insist the model's death was an accident, the lawyer said. "We have a very serious and difficult case, and it's a tragedy no matter how it turns out," he observed.

Werksman also predicted the old rape charge in Ohio his client was acquitted of wouldn't have any bearing on the current proceedings. That was "ancient history," he said.

About the middle of December, Linda's grieving family absorbed yet another double blow to their already battered emotions and sensitivities. The long-awaited coroner's report was issued. The coroner ruled that the young model's death was a homicide and confirmed that she died by asphyxiation. The report also disclosed she had enough alcohol in her system to be way over the legal limit for driving in California, and she was sexually assaulted before her death.

Linda died as the result of asphyxiation caused by pressure on the neck and body that cut the air flow to her lungs. Her neck and some nearby areas of her body were crushed, and hemorrhages occurred around the throat. Carrier described the condition as one of the indicators of strangulation.

"It's consistent with somebody sitting on somebody or somebody laying on somebody," he explained. "It could have been a forearm, or it could have been hands.'' Put quite simply, according to Carrier, the model had the breath squeezed out of her.

Although none of the investigators made a public point of the development, the manner of death raised an intriguing parallel with the Ohio supermarket clerk's description of her reputed rape roughly two decades earlier. According to the story the petite woman told sex crime investigators, her lawyer, and the judge in Columbus, Rathbun wrestled her to the floor and sprawled on top of her. She was trapped under the strapping big man, helpless as a bug flipped on its back.

Carrier said he didn't know the nature of the sexual assault on Linda. Nor would he elaborate on the reasons for describing it as a "sexual assault," instead of possible consensual sex. The coroner's spokesman said the Sheriff's Department had asked him to withhold certain information.

But he did rule out the gruesome possibility Linda was buried alive. "That does not appear to be the case," he remarked. Asked about reports Linda may have been tied up, the coroner's spokesman said he didn't know the answer to that question.

The slaying probe was still progressing, and twenty Sheriff's Department investigators continued to work on the case. But one Hermosa Beach detective had already been dumped from the investigation because he allegedly leaked some choice tidbits of news to the media, and everyone still involved was treading softly in efforts to avoid similar problems.

To the model's survivors in the South Bay, the new revelations in the coroner's report were devastating news. Disclosure that her system was loaded with alcohol was especially painful.

Willette said it was "so far out of character for a professional model, especially someone like Linda (to have been drinking so heavily) . . . that in my opinion it is highly suspect." He added that although Linda may have occasionally taken a drink, he didn't believe she would ever drink when she was on a photo shoot, and especially when she was in such an isolated area.

People who knew Linda agreed with Willette. She was way too smart to willingly have been doing any serious drinking during the photo shoot. In addition to all that, she still had a busy day planned after the forest shoots that included an 8 P.M. appointment for another job. Furthermore, Linda's body and her health were too important to her to risk damaging by intemperate drinking. On one of the questionnaires she filled out for *Blast!* magazine, she wrote that her most embarrassing moment occurred when she drank a bit too much at a corporate Christmas party. On another questionnaire for the same magazine, she wrote she was most embarrassed when she lost her top during a swimsuit shoot at a public beach.

Kay brought up an intriguing possibility to explain the baffling development disclosed by the coroner's report when he observed at a press conference that the process of decomposition produces alcohol in bodies and that might have played a role in the results of the laboratory tests. The same theory was also raised to explain the high alcohol level in the remains of an American Airlines pilot whose jet crashed in the mountains of Colombia, killing 160 passengers and crew members.

Privately, some experts dismissed Kay's suggestion as too far-fetched, however. Large amounts of alcohol are produced by bodies that are in advanced states of decomposition, usually after lying for a long time in hot, moist conditions. Temperatures in the forest wilderness where Linda's body was buried were cooler and very little decomposition had occurred. If any alcohol production took place due to decomposition, it would have been very little.

The laboratory tests nevertheless turned up a blood alcohol level that was a whopping 0.13 percent, well over the 0.08 percent necessary to indicate drunken driving according to California law. The question of exactly why the tests turned up such a high blood alcohol level was still to be conclusively answered. And it was one of the perplexing early puzzles tied to the case.

But police cautioned against assuming that because the model had a high content of alcohol in her body, she did something to make herself vulnerable. At that point, only two people knew all the details about what really happened in the forest. One was dead, and the other had one of the best criminal defense lawyers in Los Angeles doing his talking for him.

"I know Linda was careful, but I don't know how this happened," her mother told Associated Press. "We know that the lawyers are handling it, and justice will be done, and the rights will not be violated," she said. Mrs. Sobek added in other remarks that although she knew she couldn't bring her daughter back, she wanted the killer "to pay for what he's done."

Willette said the family was also checking out what legal steps they could take to ensure that Rathbun didn't make any money from the death of their daughter. No one wished to see the man accused of killing Linda paid for exclusive television interviews, selling his own videotapes, peddling unpublished photos of her, or signing big-buck book contracts. O. J. Simpson's ready entrepreneurship marketing books, videotapes, statues of himself, and exclusive rights to cover his victory party after his double-murder trial was still fresh in everyone's mind.

Unsurprisingly, Rathbun's new lawyer wasn't pleased with the way the case was being handled by legal authorities. He said he couldn't comment about the results of the autopsy until he received a final report from the coroner—expected in about ten days—but he complained about the media statement. "They should release their results in a report—not in a press conference," Werksman claimed. "I don't think they should be waging a hysteria campaign against Charles Rathbun in the press. They should be introducing evidence in court."

Kay also refused further comment about the autopsy results until he received a copy of the final report. He also continued to hold off on announcing a final decision about the death penalty. ''I can't decide anything about extra charges until I get the coroner's report—until I get it and study it,'' he told reporters.

Based on the revelation that the model was sexually assaulted, prosecutors could cite the abuse as a special circumstance accompanying the murder charge in order to qualify it as a death penalty case. Kay and Bowman wouldn't be the only people whose opinions were considered when it was time to make a decision on the issue of whether or not to reshape the prosecution as a capital murder case, however. A Special Circumstances Committee is set up as part of the operation of the DA's Office to confer with individual prosecutors, study the facts available, and make death penalty decisions.

For the time being, only the limited details released in the public statement were available to the press. But there was too much interest in the case to keep more information from finding its way into print or on the air for very long, and loathsome new facts rapidly began to dribble out. One of the most unpleasant was revelation that the alleged sexual abuse involved penetration of the anus with some kind of inanimate object.

The news was growing increasingly more gruesome, and in Ohio and elsewhere around the country where members of the photographer's family had setttled, they were also trying to deal with the notoriety and shock. The Rathbuns were typical of many families in modern-day America and were spread out across the country. Charles lived in California, his father was in Ohio, a sister lived in Rhode Island, his lawyer brother was in Washington, D. C., and his mother was in Florida.

The suspect's seventy-one-year-old father, who was remarried, retired, and living in Reynoldsburg, an eastern suburb of Columbus, told the *Columbus Dispatch* he couldn't believe his son was connected to the disappearance of the California model.

"I always considered myself very fortunate because Chuck never used drugs and was never convicted of anything," he said. On the surface it appeared to be an oddly phrased statement, unless the rape charge and acquittal were considered.

But nothing like the rapidly burgeoning horror in California had ever touched the hardworking family before, and it was difficult to deal with. Journalists from Ohio, Michigan, and California were telephoning local police and pestering anyone they could find who knew the suddenly notorious freelance photographer when he lived in the Columbus area—including his father and the older man's neighbors.

When a cub reporter from *The Lantern* showed up in Reynoldsburg and began poking around, the accused killer's father was nowhere to be found. He didn't answer the door when Greg Sowinski rang his doorbell, and neighbors reported they saw a moving truck outside the apartment a day or two earlier. But the harried retiree's white Mazda SE5 was still parked in its regular space.

A written statement from the family was at last prepared and issued to the press by the photographer's older lawyer brother. It read: "The Charles Rathbun we've read about in the papers and seen on the news is completely at odds with the Charles Rathbun we know.

"The Charles Rathbun we know is a sensitive and gentle person who would never cause harm to another. We, and those who know him, are standing by him throughout this tragedy. We believe this was a tragic accident, and support him and love him."

TEN

Preliminaries

The murder suspect's brother provided a practical demonstration of family backing to bolster the public statement of support, by taking steps to serve as legal counsel in civil matters, including a wrongful death suit filed by Linda's parents.

Robert Rathbun, Jr., was an inactive member of the California bar, according to a proposed order Werksman sought from the court to permit the older brother to meet in the attorney interview room with the trouble burdened murder defendant. Werksman asked that the privileges be granted to the Washington lawyer either on grounds he was counsel in the civil litigation, or that he was a material witness based on his knowledge of the defendant's background and personal history.

The petition was merely one among a flutter of motions and other legal filings that continued to rain down on the court from both sides in the case.

Werksman referred to the recent Simpson case in one of the pleadings, asking that Rathbun be permitted to appear at future hearings during the preliminary proceedings wearing civilian clothes and without shackles. The lawyer claimed his client's ''constant exposure in court and in the media as a shackled prisoner in county jail clothing,'' jeopardized his right to a fair trial. Werksman said he realized normal procedure during preliminary hearings requires prisoners to dress in institutional wear but pointed out in the high-profile Simpson case the defendant was allowed to wear his own clothing. The Rathbun proceeding was also the subject of enormous pretrial publicity and wasn't a normal case, the lawyer added.

It isn't unusual for defense attorneys to introduce similar motions during criminal proceedings. The reasoning behind it generally contends that jail uniforms and manacles unfairly remind everyone the defendant is in custody and carries an appearance of guilt. That's why defendants are usually allowed to wear civilian clothes without the presence of manacles during their trials. During preliminary proceedings, however, there is no jury present and judges are considered to be sufficiently professional to avoid being influenced by the dress of defendants or by the presence of cuffs and chains. The motions, along with others, were taken under consideration.

While the legal justice system was slowly cranking up in the courts and smoothing the way for the beginning of the photographer's trial, homicide task force investigators, supported by a company of criminalists, forensic pathologists, and laboratory technicians, continued doing the spade work in the challenging case. The prosecution team, backed by its own investigators and staff as well as by task force detectives, was also busy collecting information and assembling facts.

Detectives knocked on doors, interviewing dozens of models, magazine editors, advertising executives, other photographers, neighbors, and former employers and colleagues of the murder defendant. They examined telephone records, job vouchers, loan documents for the Lexus; followed up more than four hundred clues and tips provided by citizens who called a special 800-number hotline; and they poured over the dusty files of old cases that were unsolved but unforgotten. Some of the tasks were agonizingly tedious, but all the work was important.

So many tips and requests for information were being phoned in for awhile that the Sheriff's Department brought in extra personnel to field the around-the-clock calls. They tied up eight telephone lines for days, and media calls were recorded from as far away as London, England.

Subpoenas were prepared to follow up on important elements of the paper trails of both the suspect and the victim, including Linda's checking account with Wells Fargo, and Rathbun's employment records from the Petersen Publishing Company. A squad of detectives drove to the publisher's high-rise offices to look around and check out Rathbun's old employment files, talk to people who had worked with him, and peek at photo records. They were especially looking for possible links between the photographer and Kimberly Pandelios.

An especially interesting tidbit originated with the publisher of *AutoWeek*, the magazine Rathbun said he was working for when he checked out the Lexus he used to drive Linda into the wilderness for the shoot. Leon Mandel said he didn't know why Linda was taken along on the job because his magazine doesn't use shots of vehicles with models. Rathbun and the Detroit-based magazine's art director had agreed during a telephone conversation the photos would be shot in a rural setting, possibly with horses. When that didn't work out, Mandel said Rathbun suggested a different rural setting, probably something with cows in it. The magazine executive stressed that *AutoWeek* never used models because readers want pictures that show the entire vehicle without obstructions. They want to see the sheet metal.

That sounded reasonable. An action shot would focus on the movement and operation of the vehicle, and the vehicle itself. It wouldn't matter who was driving it. If the driver appeared at all in the photos, he or she would most likely be unidentifiable. And the photos probably wouldn't show if the driver was wearing a swimsuit, or was covered head to toe.

When reporters approached Werksman with the information that *AutoWeek* didn't use models, he pointed out his client worked as a freelancer for various publications. Rathbun might have arranged for the girl to pose in order to shoot additional photos to be peddled to other publications, the lawyer suggested. Rathbun's former agent also said it was plausible to believe the photographer might have brought the model along because he was planning on multiple sales to different magazines. The agent asked not to be identified.

Near the end of February the April issue of *Truckin'* magazine was distributed to newstands with Linda's picture on the cover. The "Special Heavy Haulers" edition carried a note scrawled across the lower right-hand corner that read: "In memory of Linda Sobek."

The cover picture of Linda, and a smaller one inside showing her standing next to the cab of the customized 1996 Ford truck wearing a cap and a man's big white shirt pulled loosely over her bikini top. The magazine also printed pictures inside in black and white of the six previous covers of *Truckin'* and *MiniTruckin'*, which Linda posed for. Pictures of other sexy models in flimsy bikinis or thongs were spotted here and there throughout the magazine.

Editor Steve Stillwell wrote in an editorial that the staff agonized over the decision whether or not to run Linda's final cover photo because of the notoriety surrounding her death. But Linda's mother made the decision, he said. She advised the people at *Truckin'* that modeling was her daughter's chosen career, and she was proud of her. Mrs. Sobek requested that they add the memorial message about Linda on the cover, he said.

Another magazine was also published shortly after Linda's death by Ashley Communications, which put together a collection of her photos from *Swimsuit Posters*

magazine and its sister publication, *Blast!* The special
issue forty-six-page magazine, titled "LINDA SOBEK,
1968—1995: DEATH OF OUR MODEL," featured
twenty-nine color photos of Linda, along with pictures
from her memorial service, biographical information,
and remarks from some of her model friends. The cover
shot showed Linda wearing a green bikini and sitting on
the sand facing the camera with her hands between her
knees.

Most of the photos were taken by the publisher, Brian
Ashley. He said she was one of the favorite models of
the magazine readers, and her photos appeared in twenty
issues. Like the publishers of *Truckin',* Ashley told reporters he consulted with Linda's family while he was
assembling the special issue. An advertisement for the
"Linda Sobek Family Fund" was included in the magazine.

Brentwood Home Video also announced that the exercise tape Linda starred in was available for purchase
through an 800-number and stated that half of the gross
profits would be donated to the Sobek Family Fund.

Weeks earlier, long before the tributes to Linda were
published by her former associates in the auto magazine
and pinup business, she made the cover of *People.* Small
photos of Ivana Trump and Candice Bergen with her late
husband, movie director Louis Malle, also appeared on
the cover, along with shots of Rathbun and of officers
carrying Linda's body from the forest grave. But a large
close-up of Linda's smiling face framed by one arm held
over her head, and a glorious shock of her rich blond
hair, dominated the front page. Inside the magazine, she
was the subject of a five-page spread illustrated with
additional photographs.

Ironically, being featured so prominently in the high-
circulation, general interest magazine was the kind of
breakthrough and potential springboard to opportunity
any ambitious model could be expected to give their
eyeteeth for. But Linda would never have a chance to

capitalize on the showpiece magazine spread and the national publicity and attention she had at last received. Nor would Kim Pandelios, whose photograph also appeared in the *People* article.

The police task force set up to search for Linda, then to investigate her slaying, was especially interested in the baffling murders of two gorgeous young California women with similar first names: Kim Pandelios, already singled out by Sheriff Block as a case in which Rathbun was considered a suspect, and Kym Morgan. Each of the slayings had similarities to the Sobek case.

Like Linda, Kim Pandelios was blond, and said she was going to meet with someone before driving into the mountains to do a car shoot. She told her baby-sitter the job was in the Glendale-Burbank area.

Kym Morgan was also blond and beautiful, and on the day the twenty-four-year-old photography student disappeared in April 1985, she told a roommate in the coastal community of Santa Barbara about sixty miles north of Los Angeles, that she was going to meet a man with an apartment for rent.

When the remains of the young models were discovered, they were uncovered from remote graves in the rugged mountains along the northeast rim of the Los Angeles Basin. Kim Pandelios's remains were found only a few miles from where Linda's shallow burial pit was finally unearthed in the Angeles National Forest, and those of Kym Morgan were recovered north of there in the adjoining Los Padres National Forest, closer to Santa Barbara.

Meanwhile, in the three years since the disappearance of Kim Pandelios, and the two years since portions of her skeletized remains were recovered, curious leads and stories had popped up. About a year after the bones found in the forest were identified through dental X rays and the baffling case was featured on "Unsolved Mysteries," a possible witness surfaced with an intriguing story. The man's account, reported to police after he watched the segment on the popular television show, indicated Kim may not have been immediately killed after apparently being lured or otherwise transported into the forest.

He told police he was driving off-road in a remote part of the mountains near the Monte Cristo Campgrounds a few days after the model vanished, when he chanced on a campsite where a woman and three men who looked like outlaw bikers had settled in. The woman was young, petite, blond, and looked exactly like the descriptions of Kim Pandelios. Although the men quickly chased him off, the woman didn't act as if she were in any trouble, so he didn't report the confrontation until his suspicions were aroused when he learned about discovery of the bones, the witness said. They were recovered only fifty feet from the campsite.

A couple of years later, on a Tuesday morning while South Bay housewives were shopping for turkey and trimmings in anticipation of the annual Thanksgiving feast that was barely a week away, homicide investigators gathered in a conference room at the HBPD to watch a video tape. It was the segment from *Unsolved Mysteries*.

"It was like a shiver ran up our spines," one officer told a reporter for the *Daily Breeze* in nearby Torrance. "She had blond hair and blue eyes. It was a short-notice photo session, without access to a phone."

After Rathbun's arrest, the Sheriff's Department assigned more than a dozen homicide detectives and support staff to the job of investigating the possibility he may have been involved in the deaths of other young models or would-be models, including the two women with such similar first names.

Kim's mother, Mrs. Magaly Spector, was one of the first people to whom the investigators talked and after conversing by telephone from her home in New Providence, New Jersey, she boarded a jetliner and flew to

California for a face-to-face meeting. "I want to be sure
that justice is done," she told reporters.

A sheriff's sergeant who was investigating the Pandelios murder, initially told reporters no link was found
between the two cases, although the possibility they
might be connected was going to be thoroughly ex-
plored. The next day the sergeant's outspoken boss up-
staged him. Sheriff Block said at a news conference that
Rathbun was a suspect in the Pandelios slaying.

"People have placed them together on at least two
occasions in meeting situations. Whether she ever went
with him for a photographic session or whatever, we
have not established that yet," the sheriff said. "We
have people who've come forward who have indicated
that there was acquaintanceship between Rathbun and
Kimberly Pandelios."

Sheriff's investigators later confirmed their boss's
story that Rathbun reputedly met twice with Kim and
said one of the meetings occurred at a Denny's restaurant in January 1992, about a month before she disappeared. Sergeant John Laurie said two different people
recalled seeing the aspiring model and the photographer
together. But detectives later ran into trouble when they
tried to corroborate the witness statements.

The detectives contacted a woman who talked with
Kim about modeling and made certain promises to the
young mother about her career. Authorities said that, the
woman, whose name they didn't immediately disclose,
had no connection with Rathbun.

Mrs. Spector also made the most of her time in Los
Angeles to talk with reporters and whip up media interest in the long-unsolved slaying of her daughter. She
said she thought of Kim every day and believed there
was a connection between the two cases. "Someone just
doesn't go up there randomly. . . . She was led to the
forest by someone who knew about modeling and photography," Mrs. Spector observed.

During an interview on KCAL-TV in Los Angeles,

she said she wasn't surprised Rathbun was a suspect in the death of her daughter. Kim was working with "someone that knew a lot about motoring," she declared. At about the same time, Mrs. Spector also told her story on the national daytime television talk show, *Leeza*, and program hostess Leeza Gibbons, appeared with her at the Los Angeles news conference.

No pictures of the young mother were found among the photographs collected by detectives during the search of Rathbun's house, and apparently there were no shots of the other Kym.

Kym Morgan's beauty was both a blessing and a curse. In 1979 the leggy blond teenager was living in the fashionable suburb of Brentwood, which later became notorious as the site of the double killing of Nicole Brown Simpson and Ronald Goldman, when she went for coffee with a man she met at a Hollywood nightclub. The handsome stranger reportedly kidnapped her, then beat her so badly it was a year before she was able to walk or talk again.

By early 1985 she was physically healthy, was doing occasional modeling, and was studying photography at the Brooks Institute of Santa Barbara. The photography school at Brooks is widely considered to be one of the nation's best, and Kym was a serious and talented student who seemed to be looking forward to a brilliant future in the profession. Her work had already been put on display at major exhibitions in California and in other states.

She was a couple of days away from returning to classes after a semester break when she left a brief message for her roommates saying she was hurrying to meet a man at a local shopping center to talk about an apartment—and dropped from sight. She didn't return to her home, she didn't contact her parents who lived in the area, and she didn't show up for classes at the school on Monday morning. Police and volunteers carried out a massive search for the missing woman, and her car was found locked and properly parked in a space at the shopping center.

Four days after her disappearance, parts of her dismembered body were discovered in the mountains a few miles southeast of the coastal city where she had lived and gone to school.

Santa Barbara police investigated hundreds of leads in the case and checked out scores of killers involved in other homicides looking for connections to Kym's murder before the similarities with Linda Sobek's death brought Rathbun to their attention.

Captain Gregory Stock, of the Santa Barbara PD, told reporters that a composite sketch of a man seen with the woman before her disappearance looks in some respects like the freelance photographer held in the Sobek case. But the man the composite was based on was "considerably shorter" than Rathbun, he said.

Police curiosity about the possibilities of a link between Rathbun and the star-crossed young woman was whetted by the shared interest in photography and by Kym's occasional work as a model. It was known that Rathbun was already living in the sprawling Los Angeles megalopolis when she disappeared. Investigators quickly established that Rathbun never took courses at the school, then began checking to see if he ever attended any of the frequent seminars. At their request, authorities at Brooks checked guest logs and seminar logs. It was a time consuming job, but at its conclusion no tie was found between Rathbun and the murdered woman.

When reporters approached Kym's mother, Evan Morgan, at her home in Palm Springs for comments, she said she didn't know if Rathbun was the killer. But she was learning to accept her loss and had "put all this behind me." Mrs. Morgan's husband, John, died the previous year still grieving for their daughter.

Early in January prosecutors in California revealed they didn't have enough evidence to proceed with a case against Rathbun in the Pandelios slaying. Kay said it would take new and persuasive evidence to charge Rathbun in the slaying. According to police, as of this writing, none of the suspects have been dropped from the case, but no charges have ever been brought and there have been no developments for some time.

In New Jersey, Mrs. Spector responded that she wasn't surprised and remarked bitterly that the development was nothing new. "They haven't done anything for three years so why would they have done something now," she was quoted by the *Los Angeles Daily News* as saying.

When unsolved murder cases are involved it can be excruciatingly difficult for survivors, who are sometimes referred to by law enforcement and mental health professionals as "secondary victims," to bring any sense of finality or closure to their grief. It creates a tremendous sense of frustration and helplessness when no one has been brought to justice for murdering someone they love.

Mrs. Spector complained that sheriff's investigators weren't returning her phone calls and said she planned to hire a lawyer to help her find out what authorities knew about her daughter's death and who might be responsible. She added that she faxed sheriff's investigators a list of eighteen similarities between the deaths of her daughter and Linda Sobek. A sheriff's spokesman responded to the *News* that they couldn't "go to court on coincidences."

On the same day Mrs. Spector learned the disheartening news, prosecutors filed a new charge of penetration by unknown object against Rathbun and amended the original murder charge to include the special circumstance of rape by unknown object.

Count One of the charges against the accused killer read in part: "On or about November 16, 1995, in the County of Los Angeles, the crime of MURDER . . . a Felony, was committed by CHARLES EDGAR RATH-

BUN, who did willfully, unlawfully, and with malice aforethought murder LINDA SOBEK, a human being . . . It is further alleged that the murder of LINDA SOBEK was committed by defendant(s), CHARLES EDGAR RATHBUN while the said defendant(s) was/were engaged in the commission of the crime of RAPE BY INSTRUMENT . . .''

Count Two read in part: ''On or about November 16, 1995, in the County of Los Angeles, the crime of ANAL PENETRATION BY FOREIGN OBJECT, FORCE AND VIOLENCE . . . , a Felony, was committed by CHARLES EDGAR RATHBUN, who did willfully and unlawfully cause the penetration of the . . . anal openings of another and cause another person to penetrate the defendant's and another person's . . . anal openings for the purpose of sexual arousal, gratification, and abuse by a foreign object, substance, Instrument and device and by an unknown object accomplished by force, violence, duress, menace and fear of immediate and unlawful bodily injury on the victim or another . . .''

The charges in the amended felony complaint drew a shocking word picture of a nasty, brutal, and hateful assault that it seemed could only have been carried out by someone who was driven by terrible sexual frustration, anger, and a desire to inflict dreadful pain and humiliation on the victim.

Most importantly, however, alteration of the murder charge made the defendant eligible for the death penalty if he was convicted, but Kay and his colleagues continued to hold off making a final decision. The prosecutor explained to reporters that the special capital punishment committee typically doesn't decide if the death penalty will be sought until sometime between the preliminary hearing and the start of the trial. The ominous development must have frayed a few nerves for the defendant, nevertheless. Rathbun entered another not-guilty plea to the new charge of sodomizing Linda with an unknown object.

While he was cooling his heels in the Men's Detention Center and early clashes in the murder case filed against him were being fought out between the prosecution and defense in preliminary proceedings, the death penalty was making big news in California.

At thirteen minutes after midnight, on Friday, February 23, one of California's most gruesome serial killers, William G. Bonin, became the first person executed in the state by lethal injection. The former Marine veteran of Vietnam had been sentenced to death more than fifteen years earlier after being convicted of slaying fourteen young men and boys from the ages of twelve to nineteen in a ghastly sex, torture, and murder spree extending from 1979 into the early 1980s that became known as the Freeway Killings.

Actually, so many serial killers were at work in the Los Angeles area at that time murdering young male hitchhikers and other youths swept up from street corners or clubs, then dumping their naked and mutilated bodies along the maze of high-speed freeways, that they shared the collective nickname. But Bonin, assisted by a handful of young recruits, was one of the most ruthlessly industrious, and confessed to twenty-one slayings. Aaron Stovitz, one of Kay's former associates on the Manson prosecution team, headed Bonin's successful prosecution.

Although Bonin made legal history as the first prisoner ever executed in the state by being strapped to a table and injected with sodium Pentothal to render him unconscious, followed by a combination of two lethal drugs, he was the third to die in the death chamber since California reinstated capital punishment in 1977. The other two, both white males, died in the gas chamber. Until that method of execution was banned by a federal court in 1994 as cruel and unusual punishment, the condemned could choose between gas and lethal injection. Presumably, if Rathbun was convicted and sentenced to

death, he could someday share the same fate as the Freeway Killer—execution by lethal injection.

On another front stories were circulating about the
possibility of an internal political rift within the DA's
office, or other important considerations that could result
in switching the Rathbun case from the Superior Court
in Torrance to the main courthouse in downtown Los
Angeles. If that happened, Kay who was assigned as
head of the Torrance office, would almost certainly be
moved out of the picture. There was even some speculation that the DA, Garcetti, might take over, although
it appeared more likely that if a move was made the new
prosecutors would be assigned from the Major Crimes
Unit. Garcetti was already the target of allegations from
critics claiming he micromanaged some of the high-
profile cases prosecuted by the DA's office since taking
over from his predecessor, Ira Reiner, with dire results.

But unidentified sources were quoted in news stories
as saying there was a history of friction between the two
career prosecutors, Garcetti and his subordinate. An un-
dercurrent of politics runs throughout the DA's office,
which operates with a staff of 3,210 people and is the
largest in the country. The LADA annually oversees the
prosecution of 70,000 felonies and 250,000 misdemean-
ors.

Consequently, with all the media attention the Rathbun case was attracting, the outcome of the trial was
expected to have serious political ramifications for the
DA, who was facing a reelection campaign in 1996. At
one time in the 1980s when Kay was on the executive
staff of DA Reiner, he was Garcetti's supervisor. When
Garcetti was elected in 1992 to succeed Reiner as DA,
Kay was assigned to run the department's office at the
courthouse in Compton—which was considered to be a
low-level post deep in the boondocks. Kay moved into
his new boss's former job in Torrance in June 1995, a
few months before the Sobek-Rathbun case broke.

Recollection of Garcetti's action moving the Simpson

case from the Santa Monica courthouse in the general area where the double slaying occurred, to the downtown courthouse, was also fresh in local legal and journalistic minds. Many observers placed a major part of the blame for the defense victory in the notorious case on that decision.

The latest rounds of speculation about the Rathbun proceeding weren't all merely the result of politics, normal courthouse gossip, or idle press musings. In order to retain jurisdiction in the South Bay, Kay, Bowman, their support staff, and police investigators would have to prove to the satisfaction of the court that the alleged crime had a local genesis. In Los Angeles County, the location of a crime generally dictates which of several courthouses interspersed throughout the area will be the site of the trial.

The two most probable approaches to keeping the trial in the South Bay, which could be pursued separately or jointly by the prosecution, would focus on demonstrating that Linda was either kidnapped or lured through some criminal means from the restaurant parking lot in Torrance; or that someone with criminal intent used false pretenses to lure her from her home in Hermosa Beach. The possibility that Kay could have the trial snatched away from him was very real, if he and his associates failed to pin down the origin of the purported crime to the South Bay, because Linda was killed and her remains were secretly buried all the way across the county in the Angeles Forest. The twin locations of her death and her burial could hardly have been any farther from the courthouse in Torrance and still be in Los Angeles County.

Publicly, Garcetti stated that he considered the Deputy DA to be one of the premier trial lawyers with the department, and as long as the trial stayed in Torrance, Kay would be the prosecutor.

Although Kay's decision to personally prosecute the case was a bit off the norm for an administrator, it was far from unprecedented. Before his election as DA, Garcetti prosecuted and lost a murder case while he was head of the Torrance office. Other administrators with the DA's office have also stepped back into the crucible of the courtroom from time to time.

The miniflap over the location of the trial, and subsequently Kay's tenure as lead prosecutor, weren't the only serious problems to emerge during the early jousting between defense attorneys and the State. As anticipated, the controversy over the legal tightrope walking with the Miranda´ warning and repeated requests for a lawyer was brought up by the new defense attorney.

Werksman filed a motion asking the court to exclude the statements his client made to police on both the day before and the day after Thanksgiving. He also asked that every bit of evidence tied to recovery of the body, including the body itself, be banned from the trial. The lawyer contended Rathbun's constitutional rights were violated because he was interrogated without first being read the Miranda warning; was denied right to counsel and the right to remain silent; Linda's body was discovered as the result of police violation of Fifth Amendment protections; the second interrogation on Friday again violated Miranda; and Nichols's presence during the second search didn't lessen "the original tainted interrogation" because the police illegally manipulated both the civil lawyer and his client in order to locate the body.

"From the moment the police began interrogating Charles Rathbun until after he led them to Linda Sobek's corpse, the entire course of dealings between the police and the defendant was compromised by a blatant, sustained, and systematic disregard for Mr. Rathbun's Fifth Amendment right not to incriminate himself," Werksman contended.

"Then the police secured an involuntary confession. Once the police belatedly permitted Mr. Rathbun an attorney, the investigating officers nonetheless repeatedly violated his constitutional right to deal with them solely through counsel. Even at this stage, the officers also engaged in additional un-Mirandized interrogation.'' The word *Mirandized* was underlined.

Werksman claimed the detectives ''questioned and cajoled Mr. Rathbun for over an hour in a blazing hot, cramped, and windowless interrogation room, failing not only to turn down the thermostat but also to honor Mr. Rathbun's repeated requests to use the bathroom.'' Later in the document the lawyer observed that when bathroom privileges were finally allowed, handcuffs were replaced on his wrists and he was sent off with a police escort.

''As the tape recording makes painfully clear, the interrogation itself was an exercise in psychological torture punctuated by Mr. Rathbun's frequent emotional breakdowns,'' Werksman wrote. ''Taking advantage of Mr. Rathbun's unstable, confused, depressed, and remorseful state, Saldana and Bice by turns smooth-talked, badgered, and guilt-tripped Mr. Rathbun into making an extensive statement regarding his involvement in Ms. Sobek's death.'' Saldana and Bice followed that up by skillfully manipulating his client ''into agreeing to help them locate the corpse,'' the lawyer added.

Later in the motion, Werksman noted that Nichols was in another interrogation room ''not fifty feet away,'' during Rathbun's lengthy confrontation with the two detectives. ''One can only gape in astonishment, then, at the pure gall of Detective Saldana when, near the end of this grossly unconstitutional interrogation, he assures Mr. Rathbun that unlike some cops, he doesn't 'play that way,' '' Werksman declared.

The lengthy document drew a vividly chilling picture of a vulnerable man taken advantage of by ruthlessly determined police, who bulldozed their way over a defendant's constitutional rights. Saldana and Bice weren't exactly pictured as KGB thugs or jackbooted Gestapo psychopaths, but judging from the motion, they weren't the kind of people who showed great concern for the

more fragile sensitivities of accused killers or for some
of their constitutional rights. The defense lawyer had
produced a shocking portrayal of police run amok, and
he wasn't finished.

He went on to dispute the versions of Detectives Saldana and Menart about their involvement with Rathbun
and the events immediately leading up to the helicopter
search for the model's body on the Friday after Thanksgiving. Werksman claimed that on Friday morning after
Rathbun's wrists were sutured at the hospital, Saldana
compounded the initial transgression committed
Wednesday night and began pushing once more for help
in a helicopter search for the body.

The lawyer asserted that Rathbun again said he
wanted legal counsel before helping with a search. "I'm
willing to help you an [sic] any way I can. I will like to
verbally hear that from my attorney that you will like
me to cooperate with you . . ." Werksman quoted him
as telling the detective. Saldana refused the request,
claiming it was impossible at that time to talk with a
lawyer, and continued to pester Rathbun to help in the
search for the body.

Consequently, Rathbun agreed to help and was lifted
by helicopter to the ranger station in the national forest.
There, the suspect who was "still dazed from his attempted suicide" was subjected to yet another improper
interrogation without being given a Miranda warning
and without benefit of legal counsel, the lawyer added.

Nichols was also depicted in the scathing diatribe as
a victim of police manipulation and bulldozing. Werksman claimed that for awhile police detained Nichols and
"held the shadow of a potential criminal charge over his
head," and didn't allow him to see his client until Rathbun had already broken down. Then they gave the lawyer the "bum's rush."

Werksman said Nichols made strong efforts to get out
of the case, and knew he was "hopelessly compromised.
But the police kept him on the string. They lied to him

about the unavailability of a public defender to take over the case, lied to him again about his client volunteering to help find Ms. Sobek's body, then pushed him into acquiescing in a search.'' Investigators used the civil lawyer ''as a fig leaf to cover their gross pattern of unconstitutional conduct,'' Werksman contended.

Even though it wasn't unexpected, the lengthy motion, which included statements from Werksman, Nichols, and Marpet, was a jarring development for the prosecution. It was all part of the frustrating hairsplitting and murky legal scholasticism tied to Miranda and the exclusionary rule which are so often used in criminal trials to permit conclusive evidence of guilt to be withheld from juries. Defendants who have given statements to police routinely experience a change of heart after talking to their lawyers, and seek to have them suppressed. Most of the time they lose.

Werksman and Kay were fully aware that the court's ruling on the defense challenge to the statement could be crucial to the outcome of the case. If the motion was successful, the prosecution could conceivably be so seriously crippled their chances of winning would be significantly diminished.

The motion appeared to be framed on manifestly solid grounds. Many prosecutors and police may dislike the Miranda requirement, but it is nevertheless a solidly established element of the system. One of the quirks of the legal system, though is the ability of lawyers to be able most of the time to ferret out chinks, loopholes, or exceptions in even the most carefully written laws, judicial rules, and high court opinions. Sometimes those loopholes even work in favor of the State.

Kay had already dug out his exception and he filed a strong rebuttal to counter the defense motion. The prosecutor conceded Rathbun wasn't informed of his Miranda rights and his repeated requests for an attorney were ignored, but claimed the detectives were working within the framework of the law when they carried out the interrogation.

In a thick eighty-page brief, Kay cited the "public safety exception," a court-approved rule that permits fudging on Miranda when police believe it is necessary in order to save a life. If someone has been kidnapped and is being held prisoner, if they've been injured and are in need of medical attention, or if for some other reason a life could be saved by an expeditious rescue effort, police are allowed to ignore the warning and requests for a lawyer.

Kay argued that the public safety exception applied to Rathbun's interrogation because at the time Detectives Saldana and Bice sat down to talk with the suspect they didn't know for certain whether Linda was dead or alive. He contended that although the defense might argue Bice and Saldana didn't really have "good faith belief" Linda could still be alive because of the statements Rathbun made to his friend, Deputy Meyer, that contention simply wasn't true. He pointed out in the document that the detectives questioned Rathbun about how he determined Linda was dead, and about the possibility she might still be alive.

"At no time during my questioning of Mr. Charles Rathbun . . . did I know for sure that Linda Sobek was in fact dead. My sole purpose in questioning Mr. Rathbun was to locate Linda Sobek so that if she was still alive but injured, she could be given medical attention," Saldana stated in papers filed with the brief. "Although Mr. Rathbun maintained during our conversation that he had accidentally killed Linda Sobek, I did not feel that Mr. Rathbun had the medical training to know for sure whether or not Linda Sobek was dead or alive."

Kay argued strongly that Rathbun's statements were not coerced, obtained through use of any physical force or promises of leniency, and that he "fully and freely participated in the conversation, often injecting his own thoughts as the detectives spoke to each other." The prosecutor also noted in the brief that the defendant's statement didn't constitute a confession anyway, because it was riddled with lies. Rathbun lied at least eighteen times in the statement, Kay claimed. Citing one example, he pointed out that Rathbun told the interrogators early in the confrontation that he left Linda's body on the desert floor. When it was finally recovered two days after he gave the early-evening statement to police, it was high in the mountains, at an elevation of about six thousand feet.

The prosecutor declared that since Rathbun had his lawyer, Nichols, along on the search there was no Miranda violation. He pointed out that Nichols had homicide detective Bumcrot paged by telephone, then told the detective his client was willing to help in the search. It was the defendant's own lawyer who initiated that contact.

Kay also addressed another key argument by Werksman contending Nichols wasn't an adequate advocate for Rathbun because his background was civil law, and that police were allegedly remiss for not contacting a lawyer versed in criminal defense. That simply wasn't the case, the prosecutor declared. He pointed out that Nichols repeatedly told officers he was representing the suspect, and that police contacted the Public Defender's Office in order to see that he got an attorney. But the main point to remember was that even if Jane Marpet had been drawn into the case before the initial search, Rathbun's financial status would have precluded his use of a public defender. Rathbun owned his own home and had several thousand dollars in a bank account.

Addressing defense efforts to have the body banned as evidence, Kay referred to a legal doctrine known as the "inevitable discovery exception." Citing the exception he argued that it was reasonable to believe the body would have been discovered even without the defendant's assistance. He pointed out that nearly one hundred volunteers were looking through the forest for the model and some of them were in the vicinity of the burial site. Cosby and his group were among the civilian searchers who were planning to move into the area where the body was ultimately located, Kay recalled.

Werksman anticipated that the prosecution would cite the public safety exception when he filed the motion and argued that the detectives' own words, documented on their tape recorder, was proof that at the time of the interrogation the detectives believed Linda was dead. Consequently, he added, the public safety exception didn't apply. The lawyer noted that both detectives already knew about Rathbun's admission earlier in the day to Deputy Meyer that he accidentally killed the model.

Werksman pointed out that the two homicide detectives took Rathbun and Nichols on a five-hour ride through the mountains on the Wednesday night following the grueling interview at the Hollywood Division station house to look for the body. Then, after the fruitless effort, they took a thirty-six-hour break over the Thanksgiving holiday period before resuming their official hunt for the woman. It was difficult to believe that if they really thought there was any chance she was alive and in need of medical attention, they would have taken time off to celebrate Thanksgiving, he scoffed.

In other statements the defense attorney blasted prosecutors for allegedly trying to use the public safety exception to bail them out of a situation created by what he claimed was police misconduct. The dispute wasn't over failure to read Miranda rights, he said. It was about a glaring violation of Fifth Amendment rights.

The Fifth Amendment to the Constitution, which is part of the Bill of Rights, guarantees defendants a right to legal counsel and protects them against compelled self-incrimination. But Kay strongly disagreed with the contention Rathbun's Fifth Amendment rights were violated, because he wasn't abused or promised anything by his interrogators. The defendant wasn't threatened or coerced, the prosecutor insisted.

Finally, Werksman disputed the prosecution's reliance on "inevitable discovery." He claimed the doctrine shouldn't be applied, because it didn't fit the circumstances. The area had already been subjected to an intense inspection by search teams earlier in the day without finding the body, he said. And, in the absence of what he termed his client's "tainted contribution to their efforts," authorities would have had no idea of where to look within the vast terrritory of the national forest. "It could have been months, years, or forever before someone stumbled on the gravesite by which time Ms. Sobek's body would have been useless as physical evidence," he asserted.

Werksman had a good point. Forensic pathology starts to become a bit erratic after the first twenty-four hours, and from that point plunges rapidly downhill. Even given the temperate cool weather in the mountains during much of the year, especially in the evenings, bodies don't last long under the assault of the elements, animals, and parasites. They are beset by rain, snow, and heat. Meat eating mammals ranging from large predators such as black bears, cougars, and coyotes to possums and rats are all anxious to scavenge easy meals. And finally, insects move in to feed or lay eggs and hatch maggots. They are nature's ultimate cleaners.

Infestation of a body by insects, eggs, pupae, and maggots can actually provide valuable clues to a skilled forensic entomologist who is trained to pin down life cycles and exact stages of development. The maggots and insects can be read like the hands on tiny time clocks to figure out when a body was buried, dumped, or abandoned. But after the insects have finished their job and the corpse is picked bone clean, it's a far different story. When that happens even the most skillful and determined forensic pathologists generally have little chance of pinning down clues or developing other information about the time of death as well as the cause and related areas of inquiry. Kimberly Pandelios provided a good example. With nothing more than a skull and a few other bones to work with, pathologists were never able to figure out how she died.

Linda's body was recovered before nature's cleaning crew had time to move in and seriously damage the remains. Consequently, the battle lines were firmly drawn and the motion was expected to be at the top of Judge Aranda's agenda some weeks later on February 28, when the two sides were scheduled to assemble in his courtroom for the preliminary hearing.

A total victory for the defense on its motion would not only make a conviction much more difficult but would rule out any effort by the prosecution to seek the death penalty. The special circumstance attached to the murder charge was linked to the contention Linda was raped with a foreign object, which in turn was based on the findings of pathologists during her autopsy. If the body was banned as evidence, all the autopsy information, including the conclusion Linda was sexually abused, would go out the window. And without the allegation of rape, and unless the prosecution came up with another special circumstance, even if Rathbun was convicted of murder there was no possibility he could ever be executed for the crime.

But that didn't mean the entire case would go down the drain even if Werksman prevailed and the body was lost to the prosecution as evidence. Kay had won convictions in other high-profile cases in the past when the bodies of victims weren't even recovered. One of those was his successful prosecution of Bruce Davis, a member of the Manson clan, for the murder of ranch hand and occasional movie stuntman Donald "Shorty" Shea. The victim's dismembered body wasn't found until after Davis's conviction. Two of the sex-and-torture murder convictions Kay won against Bittaker were also tied to the slayings of girls whose bodies were never found.

There was no question, however, that the flap over the confessions meant big trouble for the prosecutors.

Among other problems the noxious possibility was also raised for prosecutors that if everything Rathbun told homicide investigators was ruled out as evidence they could wind up with the admission he made to Deputy Meyer as their only statement from the suspect.

The wrangle over the confessions was one of the most crucial matters faced by Judge Aranda during the preliminary proceedings. But it was far from the only issue which would generate hard-fought preliminary sparring between attorneys on the two sides.

One of the first matters dealt with in the preliminary hearings was tied to the blunder with the tape recorder that was left activated when Nichols talked with Rathbun in the interrogation room on the night the first search was made for the body. Nichols had assumed, as any attorney would, that the discussion with his client was confidential.

Early in December, Municipal Court Judge Mark McGee met with defense attorneys and prosecutors in two days of closed-door negotiations over the matter, that spanned a weekend. Transcripts of the proceeding and the audiotapes were briefly sealed by order of the judge, but details were eventually revealed. While McGee served as referee at the Friday and Monday sessions, a Solomonic deal was hammered out that wound up with different versions of the tapes being given to each side. The defense got the unedited tape. The prosecution team got a tape with the fifteen-minute conversation between Nichols and Rathbun edited out. Even though each side accepted their versions of the tape, the matter wasn't necessarily permanently laid to rest. It was up to the defense to make a decision whether or not to renew its challenge to the taped statement later in the proceedings.

Kay laid much of the responsibility for the mistake on the unfamiliarity of task force detectives with the layout and practices at the Hollywood station. All the officers involved in the matter subsequently signed statements affirming that they had not listened to the tape, he said.

In a last-chance effort to prevent an expensive, long-drawn-out trial, Judge Aranda invited attorneys to meet privately with him and discuss a possible plea bargain agreement for the defendant prior to the scheduled preliminary hearing. The judge's suggestion, made during another hearing dealing with the discovery process, was firmly rejected by both sides.

Discovery is part of the preliminaries at all criminal trials and requires the defense and prosecution to give their opponents an early look at most of the documents, various other information, evidence, and witnesses lined up for the trial. The process virtually eliminates courtroom surprises like those that are so commonly pulled off by such fictional lawyers as Perry Mason.

Rules vary in different states, but discovery requirements in California are generally considered to be the strongest anywhere in the country. The object of legislators who drew up the requirements was aimed at speeding up trials, and very little information is permitted to be held back. The information must also be provided expeditiously, so that the opposing team of attorneys have sufficient time and opportunity to check it out and if necessary do their own investigating before a trial begins. Kay, Bowman, and their support staff had already accumulated thousands of pages of documents, crime scene photographs, plaster casts, computer disks, fingerprints, and samples of a bit of everything from handwriting to blood, hair, and body fluids.

Werksman complained at one of the hearings he hadn't yet received the results of important tests, and that he was being overcharged for copies of taped interviews and photographs. After a meeting between Aranda and lawyers for the two sides, the charges to the defense for the material were lowered. Police spokesmen also promised that copies of the full-body X rays taken during the autopsy and blood typing and results of other laboratory tests on the scrapings taken from under Linda's fingernails would soon be made available to Rathbun's defense.

While waiting in a holding cell in the courthouse for the hearing to begin, Rathbun got a taste of what he might have to look forward to from fellow convicts if he was convicted of sexually abusing and murdering the model. Another inmate punched him in the jaw. When the lanky defendant was finally led into the courtroom he was wearing a bandage over the left side of his chin. Paramedics had treated him for a cut after the attack by the other prisoner.

Werksman said he was told his client's assailant shouted, "You're lucky I can't really get at you," during the brief one-sided fracas. Rathbun's fellow inmate was definitely aware of who he was attacking "and had definite thoughts and feelings" about the photographer and the offenses he was accused of committing, the lawyer said. Kay responded by observing that prisoners charged with sex crimes are not generally liked by other inmates.

It's a hard fact of prison life that in the convict hierarchy, accused or convicted sex criminals are at the bottom of the barrel, and if they are unable to protect themselves they can become victims. They may be raped, forced to prostitute themselves, subjected to vicious beatings, and made regular targets for extortion. If they are part of the regular prison population, without the safeguards of isolation on special protective units, it's almost impossible for correctional authorities to prevent their abuse by fellow inmates.

Rathbun's image had been shown in hundreds of news stories on television and in newspapers throughout the Los Angeles area and he was immediately recognizable to thousands of men who were held at the downtown detention center and appeared at hearings in the various courthouses in the county. They knew who he was, and they knew about the loathsome crimes he was accused of committing.

Most of the men locked up at the detention center to serve short sentences or wait out the lengthy court process, were hard, tough characters who knew how to survive on the streets and behind bars. They jackrolled drunks, stole cars, broke into houses, stuck-up storekeepers, sold dope, and sometimes they committed murder. But a good number of them drew the line at sexually abusing women or children.

Rathbun and his attorney had more important matters than a punch on the jaw to concern themselves with. The most immediately compelling issue was the legal brouhaha over his statements to police and the question of whether or not his constitutional rights were properly protected during the interrogation and search for the model's body.

Experienced court watchers were looking forward to a spirited contest by attorneys when Rathbun, with his hands and legs shackled, dressed in a trademark jail uniform jumpsuit with short sleeves and flanked by a pair of husky guards, at last shuffled into Judge Aranda's courtroom on a Monday morning for his preliminary hearing. The defendant was clean shaven, had a fresh haircut, and had been permitted to shower and put on a change of clothes.

Before the judge and the lawyers got down to the serious task of the actual hearing, the crucially important matter of Rathbun's interrogation and the status of evidence obtained as a result of his statements to police had to be settled. And when the judge announced his decision, neither side wound up with all the cake. Both the prosecution and the defense had to settle for partial victories.

Aranda supported the defense contention that Rathbun's statements made to police before and after the break when he was permitted to talk with Nichols, were coerced and his constitutional rights were violated. The

photographer wasn't read his Miranda rights and when
he repeatedly asked for an attorney, the detectives responded by changing the subject. The judge disagreed
with Kay's argument based on the ''public safety exception.'' He pointed out that Linda was already missing
for six days when the detectives questioned the suspect,
and neither of the officers specifically said in their dec-
larations they believed she was alive. Aranda ruled the
statements couldn't be used as evidence at the trial.

In an important victory for the prosecution, the judge
ruled against the portion of the defense motion seeking
to exclude the model's body from evidence. The judicial
reasoning was straight to the point: Rathbun had his civil
attorney with him when the body was discovered. Since
he had legal counsel, the body was admissible as evidence at the trial.

Kay remarked after the hearing that he was pleased
with the decision and said the testimony of the coroner
was the main thing the prosecution needed in the case.
According to Kay, most of Rathbun's confession was
lies anyway.

Werksman told reporters he was pleased with the ruling on the inadmissibility of the interrogations. But he
contended that police used Nichols as a prop in order to
get the photographer to incriminate himself. Although
the defense attorney could not appeal Aranda's decision,
he could argue his case again if and when it was bound
over to Superior Court—as it was expected to be.

When the motions were disposed of and the court's
attention moved to the main proceeding of the day, some
of the testimony was dramatic and shocking. According
to Dr. Ribe, it appeared from the results of the autopsy
that Linda put up a fierce battle for her life. Her body
bore the marks of numerous injuries inflicted before her
death. Dr. Ribe testified that her neck was marked with
deep bruises consistent with strangulation, an arm was
twisted, she had abrasions on her hands and face, and
her ankles were scraped raw from being tied. The evi-

dence indicated the ties around her ankles were used to pull her legs apart, probably as a prelude to sodomizing her with the mystery object. Authorities still didn't know the identity of the instrument used in the alleged sexual assault.

"She did struggle. There is enough destruction of tissue that pain would have been a definite component of her struggle against the restraints," the pathologist declared. ". . . penetration occurred a few seconds to four hours maximum before death."

Linda's parents attended the hearing, but they left the courtroom before Ribe testified about the dreadful sexual abuse and the injuries suffered by their daughter. Other family members and friends, including Linda's sister-in-law, Yvonne, and a model chum, Kimiko Tanaka, remained seated on the hard seats in the courtroom. Werksman's cross-examination of the witness, by necessity was fierce and relentless. The two women clasped hands and appeared to be choking back tears and struggling hard to retain their composure during the gruesome testimony. At the defense table, Rathbun watched and listened from behind his round-framed glasses as quietly as a church mouse and as solemnly as an owl.

Responding to the gritty defense lawyer's staccato questions, Ribe conceded he didn't have all the answers. He couldn't pin down the exact method of death, although it was determined Linda died of manual strangulation. Someone's hands were placed around her throat. No fingerprints were found on her neck, but that wasn't unusual in cases of strangulation, according to the pathologist's testimony. "In my experience, you almost never find them," he said. "They're usually very poorly delineated. They are the exception rather than the rule."

Difficulties lifting usable fingerprints from the bodies of victims is a problem that has hampered law enforcement agencies ever since study and comparison of the

unique patterns of whorls, loops, and arches on the tips
of fingers and thumbs was accepted as an investigative
technique in the late nineteenth century.

Skin doesn't provide a very good surface for recovering latent prints, which are produced by the natural
oils on fingers and are invisible to the naked eye until
chemical or other processes are performed to make them
stand out. Skin is covered with body oils and hair fol-
licles, and when it belongs to murder victims it is likely
to be fouled with dirt, mud, or swollen and lacerated.
The task of obtaining usable latent prints from bodies is
even more difficult when murder victims are from areas
of the world like Los Angeles where there is a relatively
low level of humidity. High humidity works to preserve
body chemistry and the near infinitesimal specks of oil
deposited on objects by fingers and thumbs.

On the occasional instances when investigators have
succeeded in obtaining fingerprints from skin, they were
rarely working with latent impressions. Most of the time
they were dealing with visible prints left by fingers
coated with blood, dirt, grease, ink, paint, or other substances. Although laboratory technicians and other forensic experts are working hard to develop better
techniques and seem to be nearing important break-
throughs, so far the successes in lifting latent prints from
dead bodies have been negligible.

When questioning moved to the matter of the high
alcohol content in Linda's system, Ribe observed the
obvious—that alcohol can affect someone's ability to
defend themselves from attack. But under questioning
by Werksman, the medical expert said he didn't know
if she voluntarily consumed liquor, or if she was forced
to drink. And even though it was his conclusion that a
violent assault was made on her while she was physically restrained, he had no way of determining if she
consented to being sodomized.

The exchanges between the defense lawyer and the
medical professional about the sodomy were especially

distressing. Responding to Werksman's determined questioning, Dr. Ribe confirmed that he told detectives Linda may have been sodomized as long as three days before her death. He also conceded he couldn't determine if she was sodomized by a penis or a foreign object.

The victim's ill-conceived flirtation with suicide over the breakup of her teenage romance was also brought into the open when the witness acknowledged that what he termed, "hesitation marks" were found on her left wrist. She had begun the motion of slashing her wrist but didn't carry it through.

A model friend of Linda's also testified, providing information that seemed to offer some insight into the anger that could have motivated the kind of cruelty apparently inflicted on the young woman. Amy Weber said she recommended to Rathbun in July that he use Linda for an upcoming modeling job. His response was unexpectedly nasty, according to the testimony.

"He said she was a little bitch and that she deserved whatever was coming to her. He never wanted to work with her again," the pretty young witness testified. She didn't ask the photographer why he was so upset with Linda, and he didn't volunteer the information.

Two Sheriff's Department criminalists called as witnesses testified that the defendant's fingerprints were found on Linda's photos and the pages torn from her daybook that were recovered from the roadside trash bin in the forest.

Deputy Meyer also testified about her telephone conversation with Rathbun on the day before his arrest, and his statement to her that he was on a photography shoot with the missing model and she died after being struck by the Lexus.

On Tuesday, at the conclusion of the two-day hearing, Judge Aranda, ordered Rathbun to stand trial for the slaying and sexual assault on the model and scheduled an arraignment for March 12. He also ordered that the defendant remain in custody without bail. The judge noted that testimony indicated Rathbun initially attempted to hide the fact from authorities that he was with the missing model before at last admitting they were together on the day she vanished.

Outside the courtroom, Werksman confirmed to a mob of reporters that the unpleasantness that marked his cross-examination of Dr. Ribe was only a prelude to what was to come. If Robert and Elaine Sobek persisted in attending preliminary hearings and the trial itself, they could expect to suffer through a ruthless effort by the defense attorney to ferret out personal character flaws and to chop glaring holes in the angelic reputation of their daughter that had been presented to the public. The particular injuries detected by pathologists, and the staggering alcohol level in her blood, meant he was going to take a close look into such elements of her private life as her drinking habits, sexual practices, and the reason she once tried to kill herself, Werksman said.

There would be striking similarities in the strategy for Rathbun's defense on the murder and sexual abuse charges, to his successful defense almost two decades earlier on the rape charges in Columbus. Werksman noted that prosecutors hadn't presented any physical evidence his client either murdered or sexually assaulted the young woman. And authorities hadn't shown any proof that whatever occurred between Rathbun and Linda before her death was not consensual.

"There's a lot going on in this woman's life. It's a tumultous life," the lawyer remarked.

Werksman obtained a copy of Linda's diary through the discovery process, and according to press reports he was expected to use it to defend his client. The private journal provided a therapeutic means for Linda to deal with her own inner turmoil and personal problems by laying them out in the open where they could be confronted, inspected, dissected, and dealt with. Consequently, it contained notes about deeply personal secrets and heartfelt desires that she obviously never intended to be shared with others. Some of the entries were shocking and show that Linda was neither a saint nor an angel—but simply another human being with most of the same human frailties and longings as anyone else.

Soon after her baptism in the backyard swimming pool, she wrote she had contemplated committing suicide. Linda saved up a cache of sleeping pills, including the powerful sedative Halcyon, and she was thinking about using them. She was disappointed her career hadn't rocketed her to more success, and time appeared to be rapidly running out. Also, despite her uncommon beauty and vivacious charm, she wasn't very successful with boyfriends. She was lonely, but none of the men she was attracted to ever seemed to be exactly right for the kind of lasting monogamous relationship she so desperately desired.

Some of the entries penned in the journal read like the romantic yearnings of a love-stricken teenager. One time she would write emotionally about hopes that hunky actor Lorenzo Lamas would be her ''Mr. Right.'' The next time she was musing about men, it would be her friend Fabio, the muscular he-man who achieved fame modeling for the covers of romance novels. Most recently, she wondered in the diary about the possibility of a future with her boyfriend from Las Vegas.

At times while she was pouring out her most intimate confidences, she interrupted the narrative to jot down the words *love, peace, family,* or *giving* in big block capital letters. In another entry that was totally uncharacteristic of the Linda portrayed by friends and family, she wrote about a man who bought her a thousand dollar bed. She accepted the bed but described her generous benefactor as a ''stupid idiot.''

The dreadful circumstances of her death frustrated any desires to keep the diary private. Within a few weeks of the time her body was exhumed from the forest, her diary was being closely read and inspected line by line by people who were absolute strangers to her when she was alive. Police consulted it to help them prepare for interviews with witnesses. A careful read through the diary helped them frame the proper questions to ask and provided necessary background for weighing replies and framing follow-up queries. The journal was expected to play an important, perhaps key role, in the trial of the man who was accused of Linda's murder.

Then the *Daily Breeze* printed a sensational front-page story drawing on excerpts from the diary, interviews, and speculation that Werksman would make it an important element of the defense case. Headlined as "An Open Book: Defense to Bring Private Thoughts of Linda Sobek Into Public View," and bylined by Emily Adams and Tim Woodhull, the article indicated that Werksman was expected to use the diary along with other information to help defend his client. Werksman was quoted as saying he wasn't anxious "to drag Linda Sobek through the mud or cause her family grief." But his client was facing a possible death penalty, so no stones could be left unturned.

The reporters observed that the lawyer previously said he would try to create doubts about the claim Linda was raped, and they speculated that based on her injuries there was room for an argument that she might have consented to a session of rough sex. It was noted that the coroner's report indicated Linda could possibly have had anal sex as long as three days before her death.

Her former roommate, Bettye Burgos, was quoted as saying after reading the notes Linda wrote about considering suicide, she was sorry to learn her friend was so unhappy. "I feel chilled she would feel like this," Ms. Burgos said.

Ironically, the diary could probably have been kept out of the trial if the charge of sexual assault hadn't been added to the previous count of murder against the defendant, the reporters wrote. But that made Linda's sex life part of the case and a matter of special concern in the trial. Kay was also quoted as saying he regretted the family would have to suffer, but use of the diary was a typical defense tactic. Linda's family was aware of the pain that would be caused by baring some of their daughter's innermost thoughts during the trial, but encouraged the prosecutors to continue to seek conviction on the most serious charges. In a prepared statement, Mrs. Sobek said it would "add insult to injury" not to charge Rathbun with those crimes.

A couple of days after the story appeared, the prosecution team filed a motion in Los Angeles County Superior Court asking for a protective order to tighten up the release of information about the case to the press. The motion asking a "limited protective order" specifically cited the story based on the diary.

It read in part: "Throughout the court proceedings on this case, there has been an intense amount of media coverage. Early in the case, an alleged 'leak' to the press caused the coroner's preliminary autopsy findings to be publicized months prior to both the prosecution and defense receiving copies of the Autopsy Protocol." Noting that the *Breeze* had printed excerpts from the diary, it was added: "This material would never have been introduced at trial, and could potentially taint the jury pool in the South Bay area."

It was a startling observation and seemed to belie conclusions in the article that the die was already cast and the defense was hell-bent on unveiling the secrets in Linda's diary for all to see.

The motion also pointed once more to the frequent shifting of relationships by representatives of law enforcement and the judicial system with the press during the course of a criminal investigation and trial. There can be a fine line to be walked while balancing the privileges of a free press, with the need by authorities to conduct a proper investigation and trial, while protecting the rights of the defendant.

Early in the investigation after Linda was first reported missing, the media was a big help to authorities in publicizing the search. Media reports on the story were important factors in early discovery of Linda's parked car, and made it possible for the road work supervisor to tie the photos and other material found in the mountains to the search for the missing woman. Then some of the information the media began digging up on its own, or prying from police and others linked to the investigation, began getting in the way.

That happened during the recent O. J. Simpson investigation and trial, and it was occurring again in the Rathbun-Sobek case. That wasn't surprising, especially when both cases were centered in the Los Angeles area where there was such a glut of media outlets. Daily newspapers, weekly newspapers, magazines, radio and television, were all competing for their own exclusive stories in the sharply competitive media market.

The *Daily Breeze,* which was the leading local publication circulated in the South Bay where much of the story was taking place, was especially agressive in its coverage. It was literally leaving its competitors in the journalistic dust, and other newspapers and television news teams often could only follow up or quote from the stories that had appeared in the *Breeze.*

While all the scrambling among the media was going on, the State was asking Superior Court Judge Donald F. Pitts to "protect the integrity of the judicial process" by limiting prejudicial pretrial publicity. Prosecutors Kay and Bowman asked for a protective order directed to both sides in the case to comply with local rules of professional conduct and to control the release of specific information to the public.

The prosecutors designated four specific items, including the diary, which they said had "limited evidentiary value" in the case, and wanted the court to shield from the public at that time. The other items weren't named in the public document, but Bowman claimed in a declaration that if the information was published it would "unnecessarily inflame potential jurors and-or cause an undue invasion of privacy to involved parties."

Just what, the press immediately began asking itself, was the nature of the other information authorities were so anxious to shield? It was an intriguing question.

ELEVEN

Trolls and Goblins

Any homicide is an outrage and a tragedy.

Most Americans would like to believe murder is a shameful throwback to a more primitive, savage time when selfish desire, personal strength, or power were the sole determinants of status and survival. Of course, that's not at all the case. Americans murder each other at a staggering rate; about sixteen thousand every year.

There are so many killings and they occur with such mind-numbing regularity that the news media in most major cities doesn't even bother to acknowledge most of them. They're too common. In many cities one more drug killing, fatal convenience store stickup, or the murderous beating of a child isn't sufficiently newsworthy to make newspaper headlines or the six o'clock news.

Linda Sobek's death and the ensuing allegations of murder were different.

When she vanished and was subsequently found buried in a remote forest grave after a week long search, and a photographer she previously worked with and trusted was arrested and accused of murder, it was big news. All the circumstances of mystery, the massive search of the forest, and the apparent betrayal of trust were important factors in the media interest.

The main ingredients that made her disappearance and death newsworthy, of course, were her beauty and her profession. Linda was a busy, successful, cheesecake model who posed fetchingly for posters, calendars, and the covers of magazines wearing high heels, teenie-weenie bikinis, and a glorious smile. She was a stunningly lovely young woman, a knockout, who was living a life that for many people symbolized the American dream. Linda Sobek, it seemed, was born under a lucky star, and she had it all.

She grew up in the oceanside communities along the southern rim of Santa Monica Bay surrounded by sun splashed soft yellow sand beaches, palms, handsome bronzed surfers, and the Strand. It was her playground. Her family, including an older brother, loved and doted on her. She had a close coterie of loyal friends, and enjoyed a full and active spiritual life that contributed to the firm moral underpinnings she had instilled in her as a child.

Just about everything Linda tried, she was good at. She was an outstanding daughter, an outstanding member of her church, an oustanding student, an outstanding friend, an outstanding cheerleader, and an outstanding model.

But Linda was no plastic little girl's toy doll. She was intelligent and had enough common sense to realize she couldn't live the carefree life of a bikini model and beach bunny forever. At twenty-seven years old, regardless of how faithfully she worked out and how carefully she monitered her food intake, the time was rapidly approaching when she would no longer be in demand for calendar shots or swimsuit poses on the covers of automotive magazines.

Some models and aspiring actresses stubbornly dig in and fight the inevitable with silicone or saline breast implants, nose jobs, collagen injections to make the lips fuller or temporarily chase away crows feet around the eyes, and resort to plastic surgeons to lift and firm up bottoms that have begun to droop.

Linda didn't plan to go that route, but she was exploring other alternatives. She may have succeeded in her dream of riding the bit part on *Married With Children* to a new career in acting. She had the beauty, self-discipline, and determination to succeed, a good knowledge of the ins and outs of the beauty business in the worlds of modeling and Hollywood, and a solid support system from family and friends.

But she could also have been happy living a more plebian and practical future after her modeling career wound down, like that of the mother she adored. She was looking forward to someday soon becoming a wife and mother herself and establishing her own household with a loving husband.

Sadly, none of those eventualities will ever occur. The ambitious hardworking model, and the loving daughter, sister, and friend will never have an opportunity to realize her full potential. The young woman who spent her short life surrounded by love, youth, and beauty will stay that way in the minds of her survivors, the secondary victims, forever. She will remain always beautiful in the hearts and minds of the people who love her, and will never grow old.

Apart from the ultimate truth or falsity of the charges against Rathbun, the charges themselves were a reminder that modeling as a profession may have its dark side, even if that wasn't the case for Linda. The dangers to established models and to young women who aspire to join their ranks can be very real and chillingly cruel.

Horrible examples abound. The vicious outburst of sex and slaughter by Richard Coddington in May 1987 was one of the worst. Coddington was a successful gambler and math whiz with an IQ of 140. He was also an amoral pervert who lived in a fantasy world of bondage and sadism and ruthlessly murdered the owner of a Reno, Nevada, model agency and her longtime friend. Then he sexually abused and bound the two models—one twelve and one fourteen—the older women were chaperoning.

The twenty-eight-year-old sex slayer lured the quartet to his isolated mobile home at South Lake Tahoe, just across the Nevada state line in California by presenting himself as a wealthy photographer from Atlanta, Georgia, who needed a pair of young female models. Two days later a squad of FBI agents and police from Nevada and California rescued the girls, who were discovered in tears and huddled together inside a bedroom outfitted with a handcrafted soundproof sex chamber specially constructed to muffle noise. The dead bodies of their chaperones were found on the floor of another bedroom, stuffed in green plastic garbage bags. The young models and the older women had played by the rules and taken precautions, but they became victims anyway.

Three other women paid with their lives when they threw caution to the winds and agreed to pose for Harvey Murray Glatman in 1957. The Los Angeles man was a skinny loser and bondage freak who lured the aspiring models to the desert east of the city ostensibly to pose for sensationalistic true crime magazine covers. Then after they foolishly permitted themselves to be tied up for the camera, he sexually abused, tortured, and murdered them. Glatman paid for his crimes in the gas chamber at San Quentin. Coddington was convicted in 1987 of murdering the Nevada women and raping the girls and is on California's death row awaiting his turn in the death chamber.

But many other killers of models have been brought to justice through the years, and there are others who are still at large. Amateur photographer Bill Bradford, one of Coddington's neighbors on death row, was sentenced to death for murdering two would-be models, one twenty-one and the other only fifteen after luring them into the Mojave Desert to pose. He cut out tattoos from the older woman's body to keep for souvenirs.

Other naive women are trapped into the vice rackets and wind up posing for raunchy magazines, become porn movie actresses, or are lured into prostitution by

fast-talking, unprincipled slimebags who inhabit the dark
fringes of the modeling and acting scenes. The panderers
aren't always male. They can be persuasive Loreleis like
Hollywood Madam Heidi Fleiss, who is notorious for
her stable of would-be models and actresses turned
hookers.

The lesson for the young women who arrived in Hollywood and Los Angeles with visions of celebrity and
stars in their eyes is obvious. Attempting to carve out
careers in such glamour professions as modeling and acting can be extremely dangerous for the unsophisticated,
unwary, or simply the unlucky. And even women who
take normal precautions can wind up in trouble.

As the movie capital of the world and a major center
for publishing and advertising, the Greater Los Angeles
area is a land of golden opportunity for venturesome
young people of both sexes. And although in her own
book, actress legend Lana Turner denied the popular
Hollywood fable about her discovery while sipping a
soda at Schwab's famous drugstore, it is indeed possible
to be "discovered" in chance encounters in Glitter City.
But an aspiring actress or model better not count on it,
and have a fallback method of supporting herself
through a second job, savings, or family while waiting
to be singled out by the right photographer, agent, or
film director.

Thousands of beautiful girls and women flock to Hollywood and Los Angeles from all across the country
every year hoping to follow in the spectacular footsteps
of the late screen queen. Most of them are lucky to get
an occasional bit part in a movie or TV show, or to find
a reputable modeling agent sufficiently impressed with
their looks and demeanor to accept them as clients.

Even the lucky ones have to survive a gauntlet of
hungry predators attracted to the lush hunting grounds
by the profusion of fresh, young faces and bodies. Self-
proclaimed bigshots in the modeling world and movie
business are a dime a dozen in Los Angeles, and their

promises can be as vaporous and elusive as the fog that regularly rolls across the city and its suburbs. They can be even more sinister and destructive.

According to Kim Pandelios's mother, the young woman told her shortly before vanishing about meeting a man who told her he was going to get her picture on the cover of a magazine. The picture would show Kim driving a motor vehicle in the forest and she was going to become famous. Mrs. Spector said her daughter told her the man's first name was "Paul," and he used electronic pagers and showed computer listings of agents to her. He knew a lot about automotive matters, and Kim was going to pose with a new car or truck. Mrs. Spector added her daughter grew up in a small town and was very trusting.

Janice Pennington, hostess of TV's long-running game show, "Price Is Right," was quoted in another story as saying she had several close calls while following her cocareer as a model. Her life as a model was "wonderful and exciting," she told the tabloid, but she had to take precautions.

Industrious reporters for tabloid television shows and more conventional elements of the press such as the *Los Angeles Times* and *Valley Daily News* dug up other frightening stories about the perils of modeling for professionals and for eager wanna-be's. One beauty, who has been laboring for three years going from modeling job to modeling job in order to put the yogurt and salads on the table while looking for the big break that would catapult her into acting fame, was robbed by a photographer. She told the *Daily News* he came to her house to talk about a possible shoot, and while she wasn't looking stole all her cash. Her roommate was once offered a film role by a sleezy director on the condition she go to his home and practice the love scenes with him. She passed up the opportunity.

Famed Hollywood photographer Harry Langdon was one of the most popular sources of insider information for industrious reporters and for television talk show hosts. Some models today carry pistols or Mace in their purses when they go on jobs, he said. They're forced to take precautions because of all the nuts.

The virtuoso photographer who has snapped pictures of some of the most beautiful women in the world, also participated on a panel interviewed about the dangers lurking in the modeling world during a segment of television's *Maury Povich*. Responding to a question from the host, Langdon described just how easy it was for a photographer to get a model undressed. After working in the trade for awhile, photographers develop "a kind of mesmerizing tone of voice," he said. They might begin directing a model to turn to the left, to turn to the right, to throw her hair around, and by the time he suggests she slip her sweater down she has been programmed. ". . . and before you know it a model will just obey you to do anything you want."

Model Nadja Amermann made a similar observation during an interview on *Extra*. Suddenly you look up, she said, and you're nude.

The observations of the photographer and the model provide dramatic evidence of why some forms of modeling can be so fraught with danger. The female models are vulnerable and can easily wind up in situations where it's almost impossible for them to protect themselves. If a girl is wearing nothing more substantial than a bikini, there's nowhere she can hide a gun—or a container of Mace.

Langdon said the situation was becoming so bad that many models no longer trust male photographers, and female shutterbugs are moving into their place. "It's a sign of things that are happening," he declared.

Good photographers, like Langdon, know the safety rules are necessary to protect their models and because they're professionals and care about the women they work with they're anxious and careful to observe necessary precautions.

A photographer in Philadelphia a few years ago who did advertising shots for some of the country's major magazines, never worked with female models unless his mother was in the studio or went along as a chaperone on outdoor shots. The older woman not only provided protection for the models, but her presence also worked to shield her son from the possibility of ruinous accusations of sexual harassment. When the photographer's mother remarried and moved away, he hired a female assistant and she stepped into the role of unofficial chaperone.

Nicole Bordeaux, a former model who moved on to operate one of the biggest agencies in the business, Bordeaux Management, was quoted in the *Times,* warning that freelancers faced the most danger of anyone in the business. Even models who have an agency, but step out on their own to save the twenty-percent commission, can put themselves in serious danger, she warned. Ms. Bordeaux said some models are given business cards almost daily by self-described photographers who have spotted them somewhere and try to lure them with talk about big jobs. Then the agent makes a few telephone calls, does a little research, and almost invariably learns the photographers and the jobs are phony.

The agent echoed warnings of other people in the field to young women whose heads are filled with the praises of family members and friends about how beautiful they are and how they should become models. When they're turned down by agencies, they can be so anxious to break into the business that they take foolish chances. That can lead to fatal mistakes.

Even the most experienced models can make serious miscalculations however, and Linda apparently made several whether or not these actually put her in danger. For one, she broke her own cardinal rule and didn't make sure to let someone else know the identity of the photographer she was going to meet, and the location and time of the meeting.

She also erred when she left her own car in the parking lot and apparently rode off on her way to the site of the remote photo shoot in the photographer's vehicle. If she had taken proper safety precautions, she would have insisted on driving there in her own car. And if she arrived at the site and the photographer was all by himself, without an assistant or someone else to serve as an unofficial chaperone or witness, she should have stayed in her car with the door locked and the windows up.

Linda apparently made a couple of other basic miscalculations that might have contributed to the tragedy. She didn't work through an agent and was freelancing the job. And she committed one of the most serious miscues a model can commit, when she had her home telephone number printed on her business cards. Most models are not in the trade very long before they figure out it makes good sense to protect their private lives from their business lives by keeping their addresses and home phone numbers to themselves. It's safer to refer business calls to agents, or to obtain pager numbers for photographers and others who may have a legitimate interest in getting in touch to set up photo shoots or personal appearances at such events as conventions and trade shows.

Making mistakes doesn't make a person bad. As a child Linda Sobek was a good girl, and when she grew up she became a good woman whose worst so-called sin was apparently being too trusting.

It compounds the tragedy of her death to have her become the one who is put on trial. Her body was dissected in the morgue, then her character was scheduled to be dissected in the courtroom. Based on Werksman's remarks, the most personal secrets of her private life were due to be cut and sliced away in the effort to defend her accused killer. If it was true she was raped and murdered in the desert or in the forest, then it appeared her reputation and memory would be raped and murdered again in the courtroom.

For decades, survivors of rape have found themselves on witness stands facing embarrassingly personal questions about how many lovers they had, dates, names, and places—even about the particular types of sexual behavior they've engaged in. Almost always, the defendant is shielded from being asked similar questions, and usually doesn't even have to personally testify in open court.

Even the dead aren't immune from the attacks. When the Menendez brothers were put on trial the first time for viciously shotgunning Jose and Kitty Menendez to death, the parents were accused in the courtroom of committing outrageous sexual, physical, and psychological offenses against the young men while they were growing up. The second time in the dock after the judge banned most of the abuse accusations from the trial, the brothers were convicted. That's the way the system works, and the way defense attorneys sometimes earn their pay. But that doesn't make it right or fair to heedlessly heap new trauma on the old, and more abuse on the defenseless dead.

Models must also stick together and look out for each other. The advice Linda's father and her girlfriend gave to reporters outside the family home after the body was recovered and identified should be taken to heart. Be careful, and when the occasion calls for it take a trusted male friend along on shoots. Models must not hesitate to report a photographer, producer, advertising executive, or anyone else tied to the business to their superiors when he—or she—gets out of line or behaves threateningly and unprofessionally.

At this writing, the decision as to whether Charles Edgar Rathbun really is a monster who deliberately snuffed out the pretty model's life and stole her dreams and those of her parents, is still to be determined in the courts. Rathbun appeared at his arraignment in March and repeated his plea of not guilty to the charges, this time to Superior Court Judge Donald F. Pitts. His lawyer's motion to permit the defendant to wear civilian clothes had been granted, and Rathbun was casually dressed in blue jeans, a blue shirt, and beige sports jacket.

At the brief hearing, Rathbun also agreed to give up his right to a trial within sixty days, but lawyers indicated the proceeding would probably get underway sometime during the summer. Kay noted that the Sobeks were anxious to get the matter over with. Every court appearance meant more pain for the grieving parents.

Before opening statements and testimony can be kicked off, however, Werksman is expected to renew the earlier plea he made unsuccessfully to Aranda. This time he would be asking Judge Pitts to order Linda's body excluded as evidence. If the judge agrees, winning a conviction becomes much more difficult for the prosecution. That would be especially so if the possibility of the death penalty still hung over the defendant's head, but that eventuality was erased in April by a decision of the DA's Special Circumstance Committee. The committee pondered the issue for four days before deciding not to seek Rathbun's execution. Consequently, the most serious penalty he could face, if convicted of first-degree murder, would be life in prison without the possibility of parole.

Werksman responded to the disclosure by commenting that prosecutors apparently didn't believe they could prove Linda was raped by his client. Kay reacted to the decision by remarking that he didn't disagree with the committee, and said he believed that members were guided by Rathbun's lack of previous felony convictions and his open expressions of remorse over Linda's death. He also disputed the defense attorney's statement about the rape allegations. The prosecution was prepared to prove that the model was subjected to a horrible sexual assault, he said.

Whatever happens, Rathbun's life will never be the same. His most jealously guarded secrets are being dug out by determined police and industrious journalists. He has already been featured in numerous stories in newspapers, magazines, and on television newscasts and tabloid shows. Presumably, everything will be publicly gone over again and in even greater detail in the courtroom.

Even if he is found not guilty and manages to salvage a life for himself outside prison walls, there seems to be little doubt his career is over. As he observed miserably to the detectives during his interrogation in Hollywood, ". . . once you get a reputation as a killer . . . you don't work again. . . ."

Hollywood must be about the worst place in the world for someone who has already known his kind of notoriety to try and slip back into comfortable obscurity. Guilty or innocent, Rathbun has become part of the dark legends that continue to grow around Hollywood and Los Angeles. It is not at all farfetched to expect that some day whether he is guilty or innocent his house on Canyon Drive will be added to the Graveline Tour. The industrious entrepreneurs who operate the business, transport morbidly curious tourists by bus or limousine and point out landmarks where the rich or famous were murdered, overdosed on drugs, or otherwise came to bad ends—or where their once accused killers lived and played.

Justice can be slow, but the sad drama will eventually play out, and when the verdict is finally read, very little will have changed in the modeling world of which Linda was a part.

Her model friends will certainly remember Linda and her dreadful death when they plan photo shoots and will most likely continue to take special care for their personal safety. But other models who didn't know Linda, including younger girls taking their first tentative steps to move into the profession, are likely to continue taking chances that they shouldn't. The glamour and Lorelei promise of fame can be devilishly enticing.

A Closing

Early Monday morning, September 16, 1996, exactly ten months after Linda walked out of her home in Hermosa Beach for the last time, the jury selection process began for the trial of her accused killer. Two weeks later, attorneys for the prosecution and the defense began delivering their opening statements before Superior Court Judge Donald F. Pitts at the courthouse in downtown Torrance.

The front-row seats in the spectator section were occupied by members of the families of the defendant and of the dead model. Rathbun's family was seated on one side of the aisle. Linda's family occupied seats on the other side, joined by Willette, their civil attorney.

During the fiercely contested trial, the prosecution developed a grisly word picture of the defendant as "a human monster" who carried a black nylon equipment bag outfitted as a rape kit when he drove the model into the isolated desert, sexually assaulted her, then murdered her to keep her from reporting the crime.

The defense sketched a far different picture for the jury, depicting a spat between the model and photographer that accidently turned deadly after a day of heavy drinking and consensual sex.

Much of the public interest before and during the screening of potential jurors focused on the possibility that Rathbun would testify in his own defense. Although the move is unusual in felony cases, Rathbun had successfully testified in his own behalf once before when he was cleared of the rape charges in Ohio. And if he wanted to fully relate his version of exactly what he wanted to convince the jury actually occurred between him and the model on the last day of her life, he would have to take the witness stand—then submit to cross-examination

In his opening statement, Werksman quickly ended the speculation. "When it's our turn, you will hear from Mr. Rathbun," the lawyer promised. "You will hear hour by hour, sometimes minute-by-minute, details of what happened between him and Ms. Sobek." The defense lawyer told the jury that on the day Linda died she guzzled tequila, undressed for the photographer, and seduced him. Photographs would be produced to back up the story, he added.

"She drank almost an entire bottle of Jose Cuervo tequila. We will show you photographs of her undressing, of her naked and touching herself in a very sensual way," the defense attorney declared.

Discovery of the photos accounted for one of the more curious developments in the case. Robert Rathbun drove to a remote area near Palmdale with his girlfriend shortly after his younger brother's preliminary hearing and recovered five rolls of undeveloped film. The defendant told him where they were buried. Like other men in his family, the Washington, D.C., area lawyer was an amateur photographer, and instead of immediately turning the film over to police, he took it back to his home in Virginia and developed it in a basement darkroom.

Some of the photos were double exposures of female genitalia and the interior of the new Lexus and, along with the pictures of Linda modeling the sheer dresses, they were entered into evidence by the defense. The double exposures did not show the face of the woman, and experts differed over whether or not the photos were of Linda.

In Kay's opening statement, he branded Rathbun as a predator who acted out "perverted fantasies for sexual purposes." In a booming voice, crackling with emotion, the prosecutor promised the jury: "Linda Sobek, figuratively speaking will come out of the grave and into this courtroom to tell you exactly what happened. She will tell you of the pain and degradation and humiliation she suffered." Kay said the young woman's ankles were bound and her legs pulled apart while Rathbun forced "an unknown object up her anus and pounded it and pounded it."

Dressed neatly in a dark blue suit and tie, Rathbun sat quietly beside his attorneys, occasionally scribbling on a yellow legal pad, but showing little emotion during the opening arguments. His behavior remained much the same during the testimony of witnesses for the prosecution.

The prosecution team called friends of the model, Linda's mother, and a parade of homicide detectives and criminalists and technicians from the Sheriff's Department Crime Laboratory to testify.

Heidi Robbins, the senior criminalist with the Crime Laboratory, told the jury that Linda's clothing and her body appeared to have been cleaned up before burial. Robbins also said she found traces of blood under the model's fingernails, and a speck discovered on Rathbun's Colt .45 semiautomatic pistol tested "presumptive" positive for blood. The witness also said however that none of the blood found under Linda's nails matched the defendant's blood type.

The 1927 Argentine Army pistol, which prosecutors believed may have been used to sodomize the model, was the same weapon that discharged at Rathbun's Hollywood home and slightly injured his friend, Deputy Meyer on the day of his arrest. The weapon has a four-inch barrel.

During cross-examination by Werksman, Robbins admitted that the test for blood also could have shown positive results if the speck was from a potato, a radish, or a flake of potassium cyanide—a chemical photographers use to develop film.

The prosecution team also produced its own color slides and photographs for the jury, including pictures shot while investigators were gently brushing away dirt from Linda's fully clothed corpse at the gravesite. Other photos, taken during the autopsy, showed raw scrapes and cuts on her ankles, as well as the rips, lacerations, and bruises to her buttocks, anus, one wrist, and her throat. The photographs were turned away from spectators while they were shown to the jury, but witnesses' descriptions of Linda's injuries had her mother in tears and once the anguished woman had to be helped out of the courtroom.

The star witness in the case was at last sworn in on Friday, October 18, after the defense took over, and the lanky photographer accused of murdering the golden girl began relating his version of the tragic events that occurred at the El Mirage dry lake bed. It was a different story than the account given to Detectives Saldana and Bice during his interrogation at the LAPD station in Hollywood. Some elements of the original statement were retained, and others were discarded or significantly altered. Much of the testimony was shockingly graphic.

The witness described a day of shooting sexy photographs, heavy drinking, of rough consensual sex, and of a bungled driving stunt that led to a quarrel and horrible mishap. According to his courtroom account, when he and Linda arrived at the remote desert location for the shoot they were faced with a long wait before the light would be right for the photos. Rathbun said he had a couple of Diet Cokes in the car, but Linda didn't want the soft drinks.

Rummaging around in his equipment bag, he found a half-pint of tequila and tossed the bottle toward her. It landed at her feet, and he offered her twenty dollars to take a drink. Then he hiked the offer to forty dollars, and finally to sixty. She could add the cost to her modeling bill, he told her.

While they waited for perfect light conditions, Linda continued sipping at the tequila until half of it was gone. They also agreed to kill some time by taking photographs of her for her portfolio and for his collection of stock images, he told the jurors. Linda modelled for him, wearing two different see-through dresses that buttoned up the front, apparently with no underwear.

"She laughed and said, 'All photographers are the same,'" Rathbun recounted of the impromptu photo session. "She said, 'All you want to do is see this . . .' She spread her knees apart real quick so I could get a look." Rathbun said he figured that was an invitation so he began kissing her thighs.

Copies of the photos of Linda wearing black stockings and holding open the sheer dresses as they were unbuttoned from the crotch down, were blown up and posted on a bulletin board set up near the witness.

Continuing his testimony, the defendant told the jury that while Linda changed outfits, she became less and less concerned about privacy. He said some fondling occurred, and he shot some photographs of her genitals while she touched herself.

Rathbun explained away the damage to the model's rectum and anus, as being caused by his fingers before his clumsy forcefulness brought an end to any further sex. Rathbun said she complained it hurt, but she was "more indignant than anything else."

Linda also reputedly became upset when she realized Rathbun had taken pictures of her genitals, and demanded the film. He said he agreed to give it to her, and finally, they got around to the job of shooting the photos with the Lexus. He climbed behind the wheel to demonstrate how to perform doughnuts, while she watched.

According to the photographer's courtroom version of

the accident, he never struck Linda with the car, but it came so close to her that she jumped back to get out of the way. That caused her to fall, and she injured one ear and a hand.

Rathbun said he helped her back inside the car, and began cleaning up the wounds, but she was furious. Linda was worried that the injury to her ear would interfere with her modeling, and called the photographer a "dumb ass." She threatened to sue him.

"I took it for a while, but then she started to get personal, said she was going to take my house away from me, the one I just bought," he related. "She said she was going to make trouble for me." Peering soberly through his round-rimmed glasses at his attorney, Rathbun observed that he was having "a real bad day."

They yelled at each other, and then Linda began kicking at the interior of the prototype luxury vehicle, he said. "I grabbed at her foot. It became a real struggle," the broad-shouldered, six foot three, 210-pound witness said while explaining that he tried to quiet her down by sprawling on top of her.

"I was pinning her down to the seat," he said of the struggle with the five foot four inch woman, who was almost exactly half his weight and lying facedown on the seat. "At one point she was struggling for about thirty seconds or so and then she got very calm. I kept holding her down, figuring she was playing possum." Rathbun said that while he was waiting for her to "cry uncle" or to give up her struggle, he was staring at the door of the car, thinking of all the troubles he was having with the model, with Lexus, and with *AutoWeek*.

When he at last climbed off and spoke to her, she didn't respond. He couldn't tell if she was breathing, so he lifted her from the car and put her on the dry lake bed and tried to revive her, he continued. She didn't respond, so he picked her up and tried to get her back into the car, but couldn't get her inside. So he used an Ace bandage to tie her ankles together and sufficiently improved the balance to enable him to get the limp body of the woman back into the car.

The witness said he still believed she was alive, and decided to drive her to a hospital in Palmdale. "I thought I'd turn her over and make her someone else's problem, because I didn't know what to do." Before driving away however, he checked her eyes and was unable to find any signs of life. "I saw an eye that was fixed and dilated," he said.

"Had you ever seen a dead body before?," his attorney asked.

"No," Rathbun responded.

Instead of replying when Werksman asked what he did after observing the condition of her eyes, Rathbun broke down in tears. Judge Pitts ordered a brief recess to give the witness an opportunity to compose himself.

When testimony resumed five minutes later, Rathbun said he thought briefly about leaving the body in the desert, but didn't. Instead he drove to a K-mart in the town of Lancaster where he bought a shovel and gloves. Then, while the dead model's body was in the back seat of the Lexus underneath a car cover, he returned to his home in Hollywood. Finally, before dawn, he drove back to the Angeles National Forest and buried the dead girl. While the witness described Linda's crude burial, Mrs. Sobek sobbed in the front row of the spectator's section.

Rathbun described dumping Linda's possessions in trash cans and driving aimlessly through the forest before burying her body. He didn't notify police because he didn't expect them to believe his story, he explained. The only person he called just after realizing the model was dead was the woman who was his girlfriend at the time, Glenda Elam, Rathbun added. Ms. Elam was in the courtroom and listened and watched along with members of his family, while the photographer recounted his version of the tragic events that led to the model's death.

During cross-examination, Rathbun stubbornly stuck
to his basic story that he and Linda had consensual sex,
before she was accidently asphyxiated during the struggle inside the Lexus. At one point ADA Bowman asked
if it was true that the model considered him to be re-
pugnant.

"I don't know," Rathbun replied.

"She rejected you, didn't she? And you couldn't take
that, could you? You had to show that little bitch who
was boss, didn't you?" the ADA fired back in a staccato
burst.

Rathbun fidgeted in the witness chair, but his reply
was negative to every question.

When the photographer's lawyer brother was called
to testify, he categorically denied altering the photographs that reputedly showed Linda's lower torso.

"Would you manufacture or fabricate or alter evidence . . . in order to assist your brother in this case?"
Werksman asked him at one point.

"No, I would not," Robert Rathbun replied.

During cross-examination, Kay asked the lawyer why
he didn't take the film to a professional photo laboratory
to be processed. Rathbun said he considered he could
do as good a job as anyone.

Norman Perle, a forensics expert on recorded evidence and video imaging, was the final witness for the
defense. He testified that after comparing the model's
autopsy photos with those of the nude female torso in
the other photographs, he concluded they were "one and
the same person."

During cross-examination by prosecutor Bowman, the
witness conceded that he had no expertise in medical
anatomy and that one of the double-exposed photos he
described as showing a woman's front thigh actually
showed her buttocks.

On Friday, November 1, the jury of nine men and
three women deliberated less than two hours before returning twin verdicts of guilty in the murder of the

model, and of anally raping her with a foreign object.

Rathbun watched, seemingly impassive while the verdict was reported. Members of Linda's family burst into tears. "I hope Rathbun gets his due. I hope he suffers as much as my daughter suffered," Bob Sobek told reporters while the convicted killer was led out of the courtroom by sheriff's officers.

The onetime auto and cheesecake photographer was faced with a bleak future. He would never again journey into the pristine loveliness of the national forest, or head for Southern California's sun-splashed beaches with a camera, a sleek new car, and a beautiful woman to spend the day snapping photographs. The sentence for the sexual assault and murder of the model was mandatory: life in prison without the possibility of parole.

UPDATE 2005

The gangly photographer's moments of dark celebrity didn't follow him to prison. Except for his closest family members and those who knew and loved his pretty victim, he is largely forgotten.

Ten years after his conviction and sentencing, he was locked safely behind bars and thick concrete walls topped with razor wire just outside the quiet central California valley town of Corcoran about midway between Fresno and Bakersfield.

Rathbun was one of approximately 1,050 inmates assigned to the Substance Abuse Treatment Facility, according to California Department of Corrections authorities. The 280-acre state-of-the-art prison was opened in August 1997, less than a year after his conviction for the brutal sex-slaying of Linda Sobek.

The SATF is a companion institution to the 92-acre California State Prison–Corcoran, which was opened in 1988. At times the prison has held such notorious inmates as the diminutive hippie guru Charles Manson, who unleashed his bloodthirsty followers on a killing spree in 1969 that claimed the lives of pregnant Hollywood actress Sharon Tate, several of her houseguests, a wealthy executive with a Los Angeles supermarket chain, the businessman's wife, and an unknown number of other victims.

Both prisons are well equipped to handle desperate, violent men under maximum security conditions, and Rathbun's new life is nothing like the world he inhabited when he was photographing gorgeous models and sleek new cars. In 1997, about a year after he moved from the Los Angeles County Jail into the California State Prison system, the CSP was up to its ears in a scandal over allegations that guards were exploiting gang rivalries to stage and videotape vicious fights among inmates. The flap led to federal and state investigations. The bespectacled, nerdy-appearing sex-slayer wasn't one of the gladiators, but the violence and fear that is a part and parcel of convict life were indicative of his new world.

Although, in some law enforcement circles, he was once suspected of being a possible serial killer, it appears highly doubtful today that Rathbun belongs to that dreadful fraternity. Evidence has never been developed to tie him to any of the violent deaths or mysterious disappearances of other beautiful young women which briefly drew the attention of homicide investigators in three states to his activities.

A former boyfriend of Rosie Marie Larner was tracked down in Mexico, and is serving a life sentence at the Saginaw Correctional Facility for her murder.

On February 18, 2002, almost exactly 12 years to the day after the savage rape-slaying of airline stewardess Nancy Ludwig, Jeffrey W. Gorton was arrested for the crime. The sinister ex-convict and landscaper was convicted of her murder and pleaded no contest to the earlier sex-slaying of music professor Margarette Eby in Flint, Mich. Gorton was given three life sentences for the stewardess' slaying, and two more for the Eby murder. Michigan has no death penalty.

Early in 2004, more than a decade after the remains of model Kim Pandelios were discovered, an ex-convict and registered sex offender was charged with her murder. He pleaded not guilty. In Santa Barbara, early in the new millenium, the slaying of bad luck beauty Kym Morgan was still under investigation. In Ohio, the murder of OSU coed Stephanie Hummer also remained unsolved.

Even though Rathbun is no longer a suspect in any of those slayings or disappearances, he is expected to spend the rest of his life behind bars. In 1999, the California State Supreme Court refused to review his petition for the appeal of his conviction. A state appeals court ruled against him earlier. A civil suit he filed against his life insurance company, Lloyd's of London, alleging the firm owed him a legal defense, was dismissed in 1998.

The former West Hollywood auto and cheesecake photographer is living out his days among his own kind; murderers, sex fiends, former drug dealers, stick-up artists, street gang members and other savagely brutal men. They are frightful neighbors!